SHAPKA AND COFFEE

A Collection of Nonconformist Conservative Christian Ramblings

Christopher J. Weeks

Table of Contents

INTRODUCTION

What is a Shapka and why Coffee?

"Nostarovia!" Cheers to big, fuzzy, Russian hats! When I lived a year in Stavropol, Russia, a large urban city that is two days away from Moscow by train, everyone sported one of those furry lovelies for warmth and year round fashion. Local Russians referred to them as a Shapka, but they are also called an Ushanka-hat, which is nothing more than a fur cap with ear flaps. You can tie it up on the top, or fastened at the chin. These durable hats are made from a wide variety of furs: otter skins, sheepskin, rabbit, arctic fox, mink, to name a few.

I was given a black one from a good friend and it was made from muskrat fur.

I have chosen to title this book after the Russian hat because when you are wearing one, you really can't be discreet or fashionably cool. Wearing an animal on your head just cannot be hidden. I have never sweated so much than when I have a Shapka on. And when you take it off your hair always turns into a matted-down greasy mess. So much for pretension and polish. I will never forget when your average large Russian man would walk into a room wearing one, a steamy green fog of garlic usually rolled off the surface of the fur, and was mingled with a pungent smell of body odor and sweat.

I have also included coffee in the title as well. Let me assure you, I am not jumping on the bandwagon of the recent waves of latte and mocha drinkers. Ever since I can remember I loved coffee, black like my hat. In the early 1970's my family would travel to the east coast for vacation and all my

5

mom had to drink on those long car rides was coffee; she had the dark, rich, nectar hidden in her beat-up green thermos. I had my first taste when I said, "Mom, I am thirsty." My dear mother recognizing my desperate need for the life giving nectar, she slowly poured out a warm cup of brown steaming Maxwell House blend as we drove down the Ohio Turnpike: "Here Chris, try this!!" That's where my love began...a dark, hot roast of java, cradled in a thick mug, any time of day!

"Coffee, coffee, brewing bold.
Darker, richer than the brews of old.
Smell the bean, hear the drip,
Coffee is coming home."

My method is simple: I find the best blend of bean, measure the right amount, prepare it in the coffee machine, pour in water and wait. "Nostarovia!" Better than a shot of Vodka. So Cheers! I invite you to drink as you meditate on ideas about life, death and being human. And don't forget to wear your Shapka, truth has no time for pretension.

So look at this book like picking your favorite blend of coffee. I have included an assortment of tasty flavors: Random Ramblings, Politics, Popular Culture, Christianity, or my personal favorite blend is the sheer enjoyment of Jesus Christ himself. I invite you my comrade, my friend, my brother, my sister, pick up this book and drink!

"My heart is stirred by a noble theme as I recite my verses for the king, my tongue is the pen of a ready writer."
—Psalms 45:1

RANDOM
RAMBLINGS

RANDOMNESS

"The belly is a demon. It doesn't remember how well you treated it yesterday; it'll cry out for more tomorrow."

—Aleksander Solzhenitsyn, One Day in the Life of Ivan Denisovich

Ivan was a fictional prisoner modeled after what real living was like in the Soviet Gulag, a system of prison camps buried deep in the frozen tundra of the Northern Siberian snow. A prisoner's life consisted of stale bread, endless marching, mindless work and boredom...always boredom. But in that boredom Solzhenitsyn wrote, "Rejoice that you are in prison. Here you can think about your soul." Thinking is a gift from God, and most of the time in our American busyness this gift is overlooked. But Jesus told us to love him with "all of our mind", so we must think! Like a fast river slicing and cutting its own paths in the wild Siberian terrain, your mind is meant to wander.

I call this wandering random ramblings. The stories in this section are meant to have no rhyme or reason. But just as you would have a conversation with a good friend, randomness is more about the journey than the destination.

My hope is that this section will help you see new things and discover alternative ways to view the world. A chapter here, a paragraph there, I want to give you something to think about instead of sitting mired the suffocating doldrums of boredom. Boredom should never be allowed to exist when you have been given a mind made by God.

Winter, Cleveland & Joy

Written December 29, 2013

January 26, 1978, a winter storm nicknamed "White Hurricane" hit the city of Cleveland and surrounding areas with violent fury: 80 mile an hour winds, semi-trailer trucks stuck in snowdrifts lining the highway, and power outages across the city-wide grid. Luckily, before the center of the storm hit, the weather service gave the Cleveland residents ample warning to be prepared for a "big one." Students were told in the afternoon on the 25th to prepare for the possibility of a whole week off of snow days. At the grade school I was attending, St. Raphael's Catholic School, Sister Joan of Arc made sure each student had enough work to keep them busy for a whole week. That meant we had to lug home all four of our heavy textbooks: grammar, mathematics, social studies, and science. For a fourth grader, it was like carrying a mountain. (Yes, Joan of Arc was actually her name; and I still am convinced the rumor about her is true: like her namesake she hid a deadly medieval sword under her desk to have on hand when needed to ensure order in the classroom)

At 3:20 the first-afternoon school bell rang out—all walkers and bike riders were now free to venture out in the blanket of white already pouring out of the ominous gray sky. My two sisters and I met at our normal spot on the sidewalk to begin making the routine trek home. We were bundled in our scarves, mittens, and giant plastic boots each carrying that mountain of books wedged under an arm. Our task: trudge 10 blocks in 4 inches of newly fallen powder snow. Sounds easy, doesn't it? Surely, we could make it.

Wait, you also had to factor in frigid below-zero temperatures, and a bitter north-easterly wind that was screaming off the top of the frozen ice of Lake Erie. And did I mention that our house was stationed directly across from the lake which received the full brunt of the ferocious wind? So there we were, 3 shivering, blinded, and scared out of our socks elementary school kids that had to enter the dragon of a newly birthed blizzard. Each step home was like the march of a Russian prisoner walking toward a Siberian camp in shackles of a Stalin' gulag. And no, I am not overstating the case with pastoral hyperbole. We were trapped in the jaws of another Cleveland winter!

"Look!" cried my sister Gina, "It's Buffers!" Out in the distance, a tiny brown dog was frolicking in the mounds of snow, wagging his tail running toward us. And then I saw him, my DAD, MY HERO, instantly appearing out of the white curtain of snow. He was wearing his favorite leather jacket, chewing on a toothpick, sporting brown polyester pants, and of course forging tracks in his big black army boots: The Iceman Cometh! Somehow, in that moment, Siberia turned into Wonderland! "Hey guys," he said, "let me carry your books, mom has hot chocolate brewing and we are going to have some fun watching the storm tonight!"

Fun? Yes, fun! When dad was nearby, life was fun. In one swift movement of his arm, he swallowed our stacks of books and led us merrily back home. On that dark, cold winter day, my dad's heart of joy melted our fear.

This is how it is walking with Christ: though we face a scary and uncertain world, and we know that the storms will surely come, Jesus is with us. Joy is always at his right hand. He wants to scoop up our sorrows so we can live without worry or fear!

The Romance of Death

Written January 24, 2014

"*Rejoice in the Lord always, again I say, Rejoice!*"
(Philippians 4:4)

Last week, I was asked this very odd question, "You sure have done lots of weddings & funerals in the past 5 years; out of those two, which one is more fulfilling?" My answer was easy, but I know it sounded odder than the question, "Funerals, hands down." As a pastor, I have seen how death has a way of waking people up. We rarely stop and reflect how most of us live like zombies: "I work from 9-5...I go home to watch my favorite TV show or movie on NETFLIX...I wake up and do it all again the next day...on the weekend I do everything I can to forget about my 9-5 job...and the world continues to turn." Is that the reason we have been created? Hardly! So when death comes knocking it shocks for a moment, the zombie inside is prodded, light flickers in the darkness. But I have been noticing recently that death doesn't bite as hard as it once used to; in fact, death has become quite romantic.

Romantic? Yes, romantic. I am using romance here in the general philosophical sense: people are actually finding personal significance and satisfaction by participating in the aesthetic experience of grief, mourning and sorrow. "Being in the moment" is now what matters. Dressing up, acting sad and crying on someone's shoulder, even if you barely know the deceased, is all part of the sublime beauty of death. This is especially true when a celebrity dies. No longer

14

does death carry a sting, it is now an invitation to join in solidarity with others to experience communal sorrow. Somehow, what happens after a person is lowered into six feet of dirt is no longer considered or even questioned. Society's consensus is now to assume that the deceased will be doing just fine! Heaven's gates are always open.

A few years back, a high school student died in our town. I went to the funeral and it was packed; the local high school bused students to the church. And as I walked in I saw a host of dressed-up & sobbing high schoolers. The student who died was not really popular at all, he didn't have many friends, but you would never know it by the way the students were responding. In fact, when he was alive I would often talk to him and he would laugh in my face whenever I mentioned Jesus. The day after the funeral I had youth group, and I knew it would be jammed packed with confused students who wanted to hear me talk about his death. As I prayed about what I was going to say, I decided to write a parable to help work through such a difficult issue. I read a letter that I wrote, and the students had no clue it was fabricated...it is called "A letter from Yuri":

FROM: Yuri of Stavropol
TO: Chris Weeks of Kent City

Dear Chris or should I address you formally as Pastor Weeks, I have a major dilemma on my hands and I need your help in handling it. Yesterday a tragedy struck our family. My brother is in Russian jail, if I do not pay 1,000,000 rubles he will be stuck in there forever; my family is pressuring me to come to his rescue. They are crying and dressing up and visiting him at the jail and they are mad at me.

Five years ago my brother Stos wanted to make some

quick money. He had a distillery in his basement where he was making vodka with rat poison. I told him not to do it but he just didn't listen to me. I would say, "Stos, you can not make vodka with rat poison for it will kill any one who drinks it." He would say, "Ahh, come on Yuri you are too worried and serious all the time. When I put the rat poison in the distillery it smells and looks like vodka, and plus I have already gotten 30,000 rubles in advance sales. I know no one has tried the vodka yet, but who cares look at all the money I am getting...and plus it is easy fun."

So I asked him, "Stos, what does mom and the sisters say about you making vodka out of rat poison?"

"Oh, they don't care. Actually they saw all the money I was making and we all had a party with my early sales. In fact, sister Larissa says that you are way to serious and life is meant to get all you can, stop pointing out the bad things." I tried to warn him to send the money back and destroy the vodka. Well he didn't listen and he finally sent the vodka to over 50 customers. When the vodka arrived all of his customers who drank it got sick immediately. Many were bed ridden for weeks and two actually died.

Now he is in jail awaiting life in prison if I don't do something. Am I supposed to send him the money? Am I supposed to get dressed up go to prison with my sisters and cry? Or am I to tell the truth and be despised by everyone? What do I do?

I then asked the students how I should respond to his letter, and they replied, "That is a terrible thing, he needs to pay the time for doing the crime. How could anyone make vodka out of rat poison?"

Well, I told them that I wrote a response: "Dear Yuri, This is your brother you are talking about, your own flesh and blood! Who cares if he listened to you or not, he is still your brother. Go see him in jail by dressing up nice, show tears *because that means you are a caring person, and the more tears you show the more compassion the jailers will have for you. Remember this and never forget it: it isn't about breaking some sort of law (We all are lawbreakers), it is about how deeply you care. The more tears the more care. The next thing you should do is pay him the 1,000,000 rubbles. Get him out of jail; no one deserves the punishment he is getting. Now if he was Adolph Hitler or Stalin he should stay in, but once again this is your brother we are talking about. Your brother who liked to smile, and boy was he a nice guy when he was with you, and man could he party! And I think you should be ashamed of yourself for always being so serious: he was only trying to make some money. And it really isn't his fault , you should blame the rat poison for being poisonous. I hope that loving advice helped,*

—Pastor Chris"

The students were mad at me. They actually started arguing and trying to convince me that I was forgetting about the family of the deceased. "So, you think he should be punished?" I asked. "Yes!" They demanded, "He murdered two innocent people."

I looked at them and said, "All of us murdered Jesus Christ, and yet we all demand and even expect instant access into heaven once we die. Just because you go to a funeral, dress up in black, and cry crocodile tears does not mean God owes someone who murdered his Son by their sinful choices and refusal of his Gospel access into his perfect presence."

Romantic feelings are often deceptive lies. And if that is all we have to present before God, than we are going to be shocked and horrified by the future that awaits us. Only one thing matters: Are you wearing the cloak of Christ's righteousness to cover your guilt before God's perfect holiness?

"Then I saw a great white throne and him who was seated on it. Earth and sky fled from his presence, and there was no place for them. And I saw the dead, great and small, standing before the throne and the books were opened. Another book was opened, which is the book of life. The dead were judged according to what they had done as recorded in the books."

—Revelation 20:11-12

1966: Weird & Wonderful

Written January 27, 2014

John Lennon became greater than Jesus, Fidel Castro seized control on all Cuban cigars, and Miranda was finally read his rights; all of this happened in the strange year of 1966. Another very weird thing happened in that year: I was born. It is a year that sociologists are not sure if they should categorize as the "Boomers, Busters or Jones Generation." It never really quite fits.

A while back I was talking to my mom about 1966 and she made an off-handed comment, "One of my all-time favorite books was written in that year. It is called 'Tell No Man,' by Adela Rogers St. Johns. I devoured that book." And when my mom devours a book, she really devours a book! I asked her if she still had it, and sure enough, way down in the basement sitting on one of her crusty old shelves, there it was. "Can I borrow it, mom?" She replied, "Sure, you can keep it if you like." So I began to read it, and let me tell you, I devoured it too! This book is fascinating because it is written with all the 1966 weirdness included.

Why is it so weird and yet so good? Because it is a very honest story about a man changed by Jesus; without any of the clichéd baggage of most Christian novels. There is no knight from the 1500's coming home from the crusades to reclaim a lost love, no swash-buckling pirates who win the pure maiden's heart, no beautiful blond Amish lady who rides buggies & churns butter, and there is no appearance of the Anti-Christ in the form of Nicolai Carpathia. It is simply about a worldly man, Hank Gavin, from Chicago (think Don

Draper from Mad Men) who comes face to face with Christ. The author begins her story by saying, *"I must tell it without the benefit of togas, helmets, camels, or walls to fall off of, not as a costume play to believe which makes no demands on our credulity, but as a reality of our own day, time, household, and city, wearing a business suit..."* I must say, it accurately describes life with all the dark details of the pre-Christ world, but the risk and oddness of turning everything over to him makes the reading so fascinating, real, and honest.

What propels the author to write her story about Hank Gavin is the possibility of experiencing the miraculous in real life. She writes, *"All my life, a life sometimes desperate, driven, worldly, defeated, repentant, magnificent, filled with fun and love as it had been from the day my grandfather with holy simplicity read to me from that book called The Acts of the Apostles, I had been invaded by a passion for, an overpowering excitement about, a painful, always hopeless yearning toward what came to Paul on the Road to Damascus...a light shone for all to see. Such, they told afterward, as had never been seen before. A voice spoke with such love and hope as no voice has spoken to us since."*

And then she writes, *"For years I had tried to assure myself I couldn't hope for it to happen here ... Miracles yesterday. Miracles tomorrow. No miracles today."* But in Hank Gavin's life, she shows how God can enter our modern world in a very real and direct way.

What she wants is what I believe we all want; to really see Christ work. Jesus says in John, *"Do not marvel that I said to you, 'You must be born again.' The wind blows where it wishes, and you hear its sound, but you do not know where it comes from or where it goes. So it is with everyone who is born of the Spirit."* In the story of Hank Gavin his life change was so profound that she writes something that is truly wonderful when a person is genuinely born again. *"Nothing could stop Hank Gavin from trying what Chesterton said had never been tried."* Do you know what that is?

"The Christian ideal has not been tried and found wanting; it has been found difficult and left untried"

–G. K. Chesterton

The Lonely Language (Sarcasm)

Written February 5, 2014

God sometimes hides, he is waiting, wanting us to want him. But have you ever realized that people hide too? With all the wonder & worry debated on why humans are lonely, alienated and are longing for community, people fail to notice, sad to say, most loneliness is self-inflicted. The way communication is modeled in the modern-day American home is the primary culprit on why we are lonely, sad and outside community. Sure, sure, electronic gadgets have a big part to play in our isolation, but I believe people go to their gadgets because gadgets don't hurt; especially compared to conversation with other human beings! What causes this hurt?

Sarcasm, it is the language that cuts like a knife.

Sarcasm is intended to be light-hearted & funny, it is a way to say "I like you and you know everything I say is said in jest? You know I am just foolin', don't cha?" Do you really want to hear the truthful answer to that question, which no one will honestly give you because they don't want to be mocked further? Well, here it is, "No, I am never quite sure when you are joking or are actually telling the truth." So we have learned the half chuckle, "Ha, ha, you are sooooooooo funny...(NOT!)."

Sarcasm cuts both the one speaking and the one being spoken to, and boy does it hurt (but you considered a sore loser if you say so).

How does it hurt the one speaking? It is easier to veil your heart with messages mixed of both humor and seriousness than it is to be vulnerable and a person who cares enough to tell you the unvarnished truth. With sarcasm veiling becomes habitual. Fathers tell their sons they are "dorks, idiots and butt -heads," from a heart that kinda enjoys their son. But more often than not they are trying to down-play their irritation and maybe a simmering dislike for their son. What do you think a son hears? "Yeah, I know, I am an idiot! But... secretly I am not quit sure what he really thinks about me?" So when the son goes to school, how do you think he learned to talk to his friends? This is why teenage boys talk like cavemen, "Ughh, me stupid, you stupider." It's easier to laugh with your friends watching YouTube than having a real conversation!

Tell me, when a son is really confused about who he is, where he belongs, or why he is getting armpit hair, do you think he wants to face a barrage of sarcasm from his dad? No, so the son hides. And you know, I haven't even talked about the heart of a daughter that perpetually craves the attention of a caring father. Sarcasm, however, keeps the daughter always at arm's length; and it makes the arms of their boyfriend that much more attractive.

Sarcasm at it's core is a cheap way to win and be better than everyone in the house; it gives you the advantage to still be on top, to judge the motives and worth of the other by adding a little twist of humor to deflect the full blow. Paper cuts are small, they don't seem like much...but they sure do hurt like the dickens! And when one gets infected, it can really cause some serious damage. Oh, how I long for one male friend to listen to me without a chuckle, a snide sideways smile, or a triumphant tone of 'been there, done that.' And yet, I still wait.

"Do not let any unwholesome talk come our of your mouths, but only what is helpful for building others up according to their needs, that it may benefit those who listen."
—Ephesians 4:29

Evil's Genius

Written February 26, 2014

Some verses of scripture have a way of jumping off the page because they seem to be asking for the reader either to believe the impossible, or live impossibly. One such verse for me is found in Romans 16:19:

> *"I want you to be wise about what is good and innocent about what is evil."*

In America, this request is extremely tough, because evil is so appealing, so smart, so pervasive, and "Oh, so genius!" There is a subtle belief in almost any human endeavor these days that evil is the ingredient in giving something more of a "mature & adult" taste. Like adding a little hot sauce or jalapeno pepper to bring out more of the flavor of your chicken wings; evil, when applied, makes life and the living of it a little more interesting and coooooool. The campy Christian production is campy precisely because there is not enough evil added for the cultured critic to enjoy; everyone needs a seedy back-story or sensual romantic fling to sink his teeth into. The more nakedness the better. It is evil that gives the cinema, journalism and even the upper realms of the business elite that certain "edge" or "dangerous" quality for something to truly become successful.

I remember in my early years of walking with Jesus, I didn't know it at the time, but I was still highly influenced by evil's genius. It took a theology class on the topic of "depravity of man" to show me just how polluted by it I was.

In my class, there was a very nice man who had a hard time believing that mankind, by nature, was irreparably damaged outside the regenerative help of Christ. "There had to be some good in man?" he opined. Well after class he and I went out for lunch and I began to spin hideous tales of evil I had personally witnessed and even was a part of in my past life. As I told them I could feel this inward taste of delight, satisfaction and superiority arising in my gut because I knew that I possessed knowledge of a certain kind that he did not. I had secret insight into evil that I thought made me a little more, "cultured, experienced, and dangerous" than my poor naive seminary friend. After our discussion, I walked home feeling good about all the wonderful sordid stories I bestowed upon my fine young padawan.

That night as I kneeled and prayed, God clearly revealed to me my rotten heart...he showed me how sick, and not cool, my thoughts were. "Chris, are you taking delight in doing things that KILLED MY SON? Don't ever brag about those things that caused the hammer to nail the precious hands of my Son to a cross." Evil deceived me as it deceives us all.

"Dude, what happens in Vegas stays in Vegas!" Ha, ha, cool.

"Hey, I wouldn't recommend anyone go watch half the movies up for Oscars; but I can handle them because I am one of the few that understands real art."

"Why do people have such a hang-up with swear words, they are just words? They are just a way to express my existential feelings of angst...it's more about how it is emoted than what the words actually mean. So lighten up and f___ it!"

Evil is genius at getting us to ridicule the beauty and nobility God wants us to see and live our lives by.

To be innocent of evil is "to not be in possession of it; not to want it, desire it, or be proud of it." The best way you can tell if you are innocent of evil is if you sorrow rather than sneer when evil is watched or talked about. When you cringe instead of cynically smiling at the horrible. When you want to run and rid yourself of it rather than investigate and learn all you can about it.

Evil may be a genius, but its brilliance is when it plays you for the fool!

A Lifelong Battle with Sports

Written May 12, 2014

I love sports, always have, and I am sure I always will.

I think sports teaches you hard-work, it provides you with a great supportive community of like-minded friends, and it also helps you to see yourself as you really are. Often there is no better way to learn humility than when you put up a cool reverse layup and it is swatted half-way across the court. All in all, I think in a general sense, playing sports is healthy.

My problem, however, is that sports can often cause you to dangle dangerously close to the edge of the "cliff of obsession." I have found when the sports bug bites you - trivial things start to twist and morph you. I have seen grown men regress into kindergarten mentality when it comes to arguing with other men over their favorite color: "I like blue!" "I like green." "You are both wrong, scarlet is the best!" (And we thought women on Pinterest were crazy?) Or think about this, kids in high school, both guys and even more rabid girls, now determine who their friends are by how good they are at throwing a round piece of leather through an orange metal ring. Now doesn't that seem a little deranged?

But I have to tell you what saddens me the most is when people finally do fall off the cliff. It happens all too frequently in our society, and people like this are easy to spot because they have lost all ability to think and count. It is really weird.

NON THINKERS *(Federal Headship Fallacy, Muhammad Ali Syndrome)*

Since I am a pastor, I see things theologically and a very interesting concept to me is the "Federal Headship of Adam."

What this teaches is that Adam, the first man, represented all of mankind when he was placed in the Garden of Eden. When he sinned, all of us sinned—God calls this vicarious association. Somehow in the mind of God, I am joined with Adam in his rebellion in the Garden; because he ate the fruit, I ate the fruit. Theologically this is considered true truth (Romans 5:12-14).

But Federal Headship should not be applied to any other situation in life, especially sports, because you turn crazy. Some people like Superman and watching movies about him; but if they were to walk around in red underwear and cape all day, we would think they escaped the asylum. Some people like SpongeBob, but it is ludicrous to think you can live underneath water wearing brown shoes and flipping hamburgers on a hot grill. But somehow, when it comes to sports we forget that Federal Headship does not apply.

We think if our team wins, we win and we are the champions. We think if we yell louder or talk to the players while watching television, we are connected to them. And when we beat our rival, we rub it in their face because in our mind "We are superior!" It really can become dangerous. I have seen people abandon friendships and bad-mouth family all because of team loyalty. I have seen people go into months of depression because their team lost, or their favorite player got hurt.

Hey sports fans, the players on your favorite team don't even know who you are and they have no idea you even exist! And guess what, they don't even care about you. But somehow, we must still believe! They are "My Team!" (yeah, you and another one million of the most dedicated fans)

The "Muhammad Ali Syndrome" is worse. Ali's favorite chant was, "I am the greatest! I am the greatest." About 20 years ago I got a signature from him and he couldn't even stand up, his body was racked by a terrible disease. But he still said and so did the people around him, "That he was the greatest." Sadly, because we play in a YMCA basketball league and score 10 points we instantly think, "We are the greatest!" We catch a touchdown pass in a high school football game and we are the next Jerry Rice. We listen to 20 hours of sports talk a day, and we know more than Troy Aikman. "We believe we are the greatest," and so many of us really believe it!

NON COUNTERS *(Playing Bad Odds)*

Think about the time, money and effort it takes to make your kid "the greatest?" I have major regrets because I was blinded by the Ali Syndrome for at least 20 years of my life, and in that time I barely read a book. I worked silly jobs so I could keep my time open to play more sports, and I never properly evaluated what I was good at. But think about the odds of being the greatest: (Take High School Basketball for Example)

- 34,450: these are the number of men's High School Basketball Teams.

- 346: these are the number of men's College Basketball Teams.

- 30: these are the number of NBA Teams. Recently I read someone who calculated the actual odds to make it to the NBA: *"NCAA senior players drafted by an NBA team: Less than one in 75, or 1.3 percent—High school senior players eventually drafted by an NBA team: About three in 10,000, or 0.03 percent. That's roughly the chance of getting four of a kind in the first round of draw poker."*

Over the years parents will pay thousands of dollars, and drive hundreds of miles to give their kid a shot at the big time.

What are the odds? Think about it? That's the problem, we don't. And then when our kids graduate high school, they don't know how to meet with God, Sunday is just another day to play sports. And after it is all said and done they become depressed because we told them they "really" have a shot.

So are you saying my kid doesn't have a shot? The real question is, "Why is this the highest goal for your kid? Why do we determine significance by dribbling skills, passing accuracy, and 100 meter dash time? Sure, having your kids play sports is healthy, but that isn't the end for which God created them. In our quest for stardom, we have more often than we can be honest about, sacrificed them on the altar of athletic arrogance. It is killing our kids. They made the team so they think they are special (that is...better than those nerds in band), they made the winning shot so they are significant, they have their name in the paper, so they have arrived. But do they know Christ? Do they understand godly humility? Do they have any hunger for his word? (Nah, it's Sunday, we need to go to Newark for a tournament)

One more thing: the college basketball tournament is coming up, what are the odds that your team will win? Don't mean to burst your bubble, but March Madness is designed to disappoint. If we can watch it for enjoyment, great! But don't watch it to prove your superiority: It has failed me personally for the last 40 years...I am an Ohio State fan, so I know!

My final point: Enjoy but don't obsess, somehow when your child falls off the cliff of sports they just might lose a part of your soul that you can never get back.

"What does it profit it a man if he were to gain the whole world (sports, fame and glory) and yet lose his own soul?"

—Mark 8:36

Sipping Drinks on a Yacht

Written March 3, 2016

A man died last week. His name was Todd.

He had a regular name, he was a regular guy. He just happened to be living in Togo, West Africa, and working as a physician's assistant helping the African poor in a hospital called Hope. His death was shocking; his body shut down after battling with both malaria and typhoid fever. He left behind a wife and four boys. He was 46.

His wife made this statement concerning his passing:

"My heart is overwhelmed with unspeakable grief – for myself, our boys, our extended family, our spiritual family and the Hospital of Hope team. I cling only to the gospel and the certain hope of our salvation through Jesus Christ. I long for the men, women and children of Togo to know the Savior that Todd served so faithfully. Even in my pain, I am confident that our sacrifice – that Todd's sacrifice – was worth it. I believe that the great commission is a cause worth dying for. And in the midst of my grief, I fix my eyes on Jesus, the author and finisher of my faith."

She believes her husband's willingness to risk his life and his family's well-being was worth it.

I was listening to the radio this morning and the broadcasters were discussing the life of another man. I won't mention his name, but he also is young. But unlike Todd, he is very famous. He owns his own jet, owns a multi-million dollar house and is admired by many. If he wants to meet his friends who live across the country for a day, he hops on his jet, and he is able to hang out with them sipping drinks on a yacht.

This man is "living the life." And no one is questioning if it is worth it—in fact, most people I know would sell all they have to be where this man is. This is probably not the case when people look at Todd's life. I find people have more pity and offer a lot of patronizing sentiment, "Wow, he gave his life for such a just cause, he clearly was sold out for Jesus...but what will become of his kids?"

Was Todd's life really worth it? Is sacrifice for Christ really necessary when I can have drinks on a yacht? I know that it is possible to have both, but the probability of having your cake and eating it too is very minimal. As Jesus says in Matthew 6, "Either you serve God or money."

When I heard about Todd's death I couldn't help but evaluate my own choices. Am I living a life that is "worth it?" This isn't the first time I ever asked this. I can remember when my dad, after 40 years of working his tail off for his family, lost it all after he was fired. It was then my dad started asking the question, "Was all that hard work worth it?"

I can remember how my family, right before that earth-shaking moment in my dad's life, was caught up in a very entertaining and leisurely lifestyle: Every weekend we would have big family get-togethers, watch two or three movies. play cards, make family movies on our video tape recorder and laugh late into the night. But when my dad lost his job, we all did reassessments of worth, "Is life simply for hanging out with your family laughing, watching movies, eating large meals or were we made for more than this?" My dad decided to start reading the Bible. So did my mom, so did my brother and after a while, so did I. During this time of questioning meaning, I ran across this verse in Revelation 3:16,

"Because you are lukewarm, neither hot nor cold, I am about to spit you out of my mouth."

I wasn't much of a Bible scholar at the time, but I knew this verse was calling me out of complacency. It chilled me to my bone. I was a man of leisure, living for comfort, with few if any convictions about anything of substance. This verse described my soul acutely, I was lukewarm; even worse, I was aimless. Meaning, worth, purpose and even the answers to 'life after death' started haunting me and most of the rest of my family.

We began to hammer God with questions, we started to place more weight on our daily decisions—we knew we were responsible before an Eternal God.

Over time we became members of a local church, we started loving our neighbor, and as a result we each felt called to serve people in a very unique way. For the next 12 years both my mom and dad led Bible studies with BSF (Bible Studies Fellowship), my brother became a missionary to the Indians in Bolivia, my sister Gina began working with prisoners in Los Angeles jails, my sisters Stephanie and Tam began giving and contributing in major ways to the local church, and God called me to a life of pastoring. We didn't do it to earn points, or even impress God, we just wanted our lives to count. The only problem with these choices is that we no longer could make family movies or spend Saturday nights together watching old re-runs like we use to.

Was it worth it? I think so, but I still am not sure until I see my God face to face.

And in a way, I don't care because I really hated the feeling of being lukewarm—I like being hot. It helps me sleep better at night, and it is actually rewarding to see people completely change because I was able to introduce them to a man named Jesus.

While writing this blog in a nearby coffee shop, a song came over the speakers and the words were rather simple, "I'm singing in the shower." Just think, a person has become wealthy and famous because they wrote a song about singing in a shower? If that is all I had to take with me into eternity I would feel pretty silly before God. For that matter, if I was only famous for shooting a round ball and sipping drinks on a yacht I think I would still feel rather naked before Holiness.

I know this, even though Todd died in relative obscurity, I don't think he is embarrassed before God at all. Nor do I think God is embarrassed by him. Listen to what Hebrews 11:13-18 says,

"These all died in faith, not having received the things promised, but having seen them and greeted them from afar, and having acknowledged that they were strangers and exiles on the earth. For people who speak thus make it clear that they are seeking a homeland. If they had been thinking of that land from which they had gone out, they would have had opportunity to return. But as it is, they desire a better country, that is, a heavenly one. Therefore God is not ashamed to be called their God, for he has prepared for them a city."

That to me is how worth is measured...is God ashamed of me? If the answer is no, life has been good, really, really good!

POLITICS

EVERYTHING IS POLITICAL

"For us in Russia, communism is a dead dog, while, for many people in the West, it is still a living lion."

—Aleksander Solzhenitsyn

You can't avoid politics.

As much as people think they are outside the fray, they still are playing the game. And politics is most definitely a game, a very bloody game.

Let's be honest, most of my readers hate talking about politics. But we must. Before my wife and I spent our year in Russia, she did not really see the significance of debating political ideas. Elections, philosophical arguments, and economic policy was about as interesting as watching paint dry for her. But then she walked the streets of Moscow and Stavropol. She saw:

- **Soldiers with machine guns greeting us at the airport.**

- **Military tanks rolling frequently down the highways.**

- **Bread lines that were a common experience.**

All of these problematic issues were the direct result of political decisions. It really matters. Ideas have consequences.

And just because you cry a tear or vote for a person who sounds like they care does not mean they do. Never forget that bad ideology leads to bad politics, and bad politics is what eventually spills innocent blood.

The Progressive Pendulum

Written January 8, 2014

My mom bought me the DVD for Christmas: "Vincent Price in 'The Pit and the Pendulum.'" It is really scary...

...and so is the way Christians in each generation swing back and forth from conservative to progressive. Your father is a right-wing zealot, he sees politics as a weapon of power— and without meaning it, he also perceives it having potential as a path to salvation. "We can bring God's kingdom to earth through electing the right candidate."

Children can't live off of their parent's political zealotry, there is no life in it. The moral majority of the 80's are not akin to the apostles. Joining in "Focus on the Family" boycotts will not persuade the masses to turn and repent. Political salvation is nothing more than Christian heresy and hypocrisy; which in turn breeds contempt. The children see their parent's love of Fox News and Ronald Reagan as a betrayal of Christ. So the pendulum swings and their contempt turns into arrogance. Hatred of the "right" breeds a new-bright hope and a superior feeling towards the ideas of the "left"; progressive politics is adopted as the new savior.

In an attempt to save the gospel from the "right's" poison; the next generation's naive arrogance leaves them open to allowing the gospel to be kidnapped by the "left". The pendulum swings! Loyalty to Christ really becomes loyalty to progressive ideas. It is the other side of the political tug-of-war. But there often is a tinge more arrogance and self-righteousness included with each successive swing. "You hypocrites," is another way of saying, "Me righteous!" And boy, discussing ideas with arrogant people is a tough go. Just try to tell a progressive that you think it not scriptural to accept the practice of homosexuality with open arms, or explain to them why abortion is a very important voting issue, and they will instantly accuse you of being a "Fox News" watcher. That is worse than being called a Nazi in some circles. (To defend yourself just admit you listened to NPR in the last week and they may let you off the hook?)

The pendulum swings...right, left, conservative, progressive, hatred, arrogance...WILL SOMEONE JUST STOP THE PENDULUM FROM SWINGING? How? One word of advice, Philippians 2:3, "in humility value others better than yourselves."

I Can't Hold My Tongue On This One

Written January 13, 2014

For a moment, I would like to revisit the progressive pendulum swing; I will show you how it actually works in reality. Two days ago I read an article in the New York Times that has me a little unhinged, it is titled, "Sex is Not Our Problem," written by Charles M. Blow. He is a very intelligent & sophisticated op-ed journalist at the New York Times. He also appears on CNN and MSNBC—you could say he is firmly placed on America's progressive stage.

His article is yet another attempt of trying to solve the complex and confounding problem of our country's high rate of "unintended pregnancies & sexually transmitted infections." It is a noble goal, one that all caring parents and leaders should be concerned about. But as you read his article it is clear that he also means to attack conservatives by painting them as "simplistic" and "puritanical" (a code-word that means they don't like sex & they aren't cool—you will never catch them dead in a new pair of metro-sexual skinny jeans!). Like all lock-step progressives, he hates the idea of the nuclear family: for progressives, the family is nothing more than a construct of European patriarchal hegemony. In other words, traditional marriage was designed by white men who want power over women. You know: having June Cleaver in the kitchen, children who are seen and not heard, and a properly folded newspaper to read on the sofa (preferably the Wall Street Journal and not the New York Times).

So, what is his solution to address, as he says, "the

complex areas of causation" that lead to these high rates of untended pregnancies? Are you ready for his wisdom and insight, it is quite breathtaking:

1. "Teach young people to value themselves in a way that contextualizes the initiation of sexual activity as a thing fully within their control and not so easily manipulated by peer and societal pressures." Try reciting that sentence to your kids! They will look at you and say, "Huh?" And I guarantee you this lesson will not work on the 16-year-old male in the back seat of a car.

2. "Abstinence can be honorable, but it won't be for everyone." This is like saying, "Some students are very honorable when they don't buy those new $150 Air Jordan's on their parent's credit card; but credit card abstinence isn't for everyone, go ahead, spend." What student who is under the grip of hormones will care about "honor" when progressive elites so easily excuse a teen's lack of self-control?

3. "They must love themselves enough emotionally to be in control of whom they allow to love them physically." It is proven, girls who do not have substantial love from a father figure crave it from other places. So let's get rid of the nuclear family because dads are really not that important, and oh yeah, in place of that, love yourself....THAT WILL STOP THE NEED FOR GIRLS seeking affirmation from horny guys at a rave party.

And to top it off, all of these powerful lessons can be implemented through, more spending on education & offering fewer abortion restrictions. Education is the progressive's panacea for everything! Have you ever noticed how most progressive ideas originate from college and university professors?

Didn't Whitney Houston sing something about learning to love yourself? Bobby Brown really helped her with that one!

TOP TEN: Political Pet Peeves

Written January 30, 2014

10. Whenever actors, athletes, and pop-musicians are seen as experts in policy, especially when discussing supposed moral issues like poverty and wealth distribution; and yet they spend their money on their third house and 5th vacation to Acapulco. (And ironically the millions they make come from playing billionaire Wall Street playboys…and they love every minute of it).

9. When students think their parents, former pastors and leaders are "stuck in the mud politically and socially;" but when the student becomes "stuck in the mud financially or emotionally" the parents, pastors and leaders are the first people they run to. (And it is usually because the progressive voices they have been listening to are never really available to come help them out).

8. When people declare themselves as "independent" not because they really have convictions but because they like to look down on people who do have convictions.

7. When politicians say they are defenders of the poor while sinking your money into programs that increase systemic poverty; and even though you daily work with the poor and support people and organizations that do, they accuse you as being "someone who doesn't care" because you want accountability with the services and money you provide.

6. When politicians say they are speaking "on behalf of the American people" but they never say anything you personally agree with.

5. When people claim their ideas are "morally righteous" but they don't think God or religion has any place in public debate. (Often these same people can be found in progressive gospel denying churches broadcasting their agenda to bring the kingdom of God on earth, while they moan and complain when their opponents try to form their convictions and policies from widely held orthodox biblical teachings).

4. When politicians always expect you to trust their motives and show them loyalty while ignoring their actual words because they have a history of lying through their teeth.

3. When people accuse you of being on the wrong side of history and you are only trying to be faithful to the one who created history.

2. When people feel morally superior to you because while you see the content of a person's character as a prime factor in the way you vote; the color of skin or gender is the most important thing to them when they vote (and they will often say they are one of Martin Luther King Jr's biggest fans).

1. When people accuse you of being a "single-issue voter" simply because the premeditated murder of an innocent human being really does bother and infuriate you.

* *Suggested reading for more fun:* "Letters to a Young Progressive: How to Avoid Wasting Your Life Protesting Things You Don't Understand" by Mike S. Adams

The Road to Real PEACE (never travels through the swamp of ACQUIESCENCE)

Written January 4, 2016

acquiescence - the reluctant acceptance of something without protest.

Humility is a character quality that looks good on paper but is easily ignored and abused in the real world. This is especially true when humility runs into a proud and controlling person. I know because by nature I am compliant and one of the kindest and most humble people you will ever meet. See how humble I am? Over the years in my desire for peace, I would often cave into the shoddy arguments of the proud and authoritative manipulation of bad leadership. Probably one of the most used and abused verses aimed at bringing the humble heart to subservience is Romans 12:18. It says,

"If possible, so far as it depends on you, be at peace with all men."

If possible? In the mind of the humble, it is always possible to be at peace—all you have to do is give in and let the other person have their way. Have you ever noticed, the proud man never gives in? In his arrogance and conceit, he usually thinks he is right. That is the danger of pride, when you think you are right you rarely give any credence to other people's arguments and reasons. Or you tell yourself that a person thinks the way they do because they are so far below you that their ideas don't even deserve to be listened to.

What if the proud person isn't right? What if he simply is pushing his selfish agenda? What if he is deluded in thinking he is right, but he is way off target?

A major crisis takes place in the mind of the humble, "If I disagree with them then we will not be at peace. And God tells me that I need to do all I can to be at peace. But I don't agree. Shouldn't I be willing to take one on the chin for peace? How come they never take one on the chin? And plus they are wrong."

So then after the humble person rouses up his courage and disagrees, the proud person cries foul. Let me give you a few examples:

- What if a President presents a health care plan you really believe will bankrupt a country? What if you disagree with him and say that there has to be a better way? In our current political landscape, you will be called a hater, a fool or simply a person that is an obstructionist. Don't you see, you are wrong?

- What if a proud parent tells their child they must always take their advice on any number of issues? I once had a dad come into my office who was upset that his 16-year-old daughter put a different color hair dye in her hair when he didn't want her to. She was forever labeled as a rebel and ungrateful teen.

- What if a senior pastor doesn't like the music of a worship pastor, does he have the right to fire him? I have seen it happen often.

What is real peace? That is tough to answer; but I know this, just because there is agreement does not mean there is peace. If a humble person keeps complying against his will and better judgment, bitterness will start to take root. Even though he may agree on the outside, inside a storm is brewing. And if you are not careful, it may come spilling out in very public ways.

So if you are one of the few and proud people of humility, learn to stand up on your convictions and go ahead, make your argument. Peace is hard to come by, and remember is never can be reached through the swamp of acquiescence—you will only be stuck in a never-ending game of control and manipulation.

That Nasty Demon Named Politics

Written January 8, 2016

"Jargon, not argument, is your best ally..."
—Your affectionate Uncle Screwtape

Last night I couldn't sleep. I needed a good book to read, something to get lost in. For the first time in my life, I have grown tired of reading about Hitler and his Nazi's. So I ventured over to the bookshelf to see if there was anything there that looked a tad bit intriguing?

A small little book in the left corner of the bottom shelf caught my eye, "The Screwtape Letters." I haven't read that short whimsical tale in 15 some odd years. I forgot most of it—and what a joy that is. Nothing like being reacquainted with an old friend. The cover has a simple white background with red borders, a gargoyle drawing at the top and C.S. Lewis' large signature scribbled across the middle.

It was time to read. Wearing my black plaid pajamas, I poured myself a dark cup of Jo. Ah, nothing liking reading in a quiet house with a slumbering family safely tucked away. I opened the front page and started slow, word by tasty word, line by wonderful line. After the first terse paragraph into the book, I came across a well-worn phrase that has always struck me as a classic tidbit of Lewis' wisdom. It reads like this:

"There are two equal and opposite errors into which our race can fall about the devils (a.k.a.: demons and Satan). One is to disbelieve in their existence. The other is to believe, and to feel an excessive and unhealthy interest in them. They themselves are equally pleased by both errors and hail a materialist or a magician with the same delight."

Sublime wisdom.

You know, as I pondered this statement, a new thought crossed my mind. This same deep current of truth can also be applied to our modern day political arena. On one hand, there are many who regard politics as irrelevant and absurd. They "disbelieve" in finding any hope for honesty and integrity, not caring a lick who governs or wins the nomination for each respective party. They have given up.

Then there are those on the other side, I call them the obsessed. Every move the president makes will either spark an uncontrollable fire of rage or send a shiver of delight running up their thigh. They are ravenous political animals living off of cable news and reading biased right and left wing blogs. They also are easy prey for jargon, political slogan and silly generalizations. As Lewis quips, "they can feel an excessive and unhealthy interest in" jumping into the political fray.

Both of these approaches are juvenile. When it comes to how your country, state and town are run you should care, but not be consumed. It is like walking the ridge of a steep rooftop; if you lean too far one way or the other you could topple off and hurt yourself and others. This is exactly the reason why people are warned never to talk about "politics and religion" when sitting at a table of strangers. Once the phrase "What think ye of the President?" is let out of Pandora's locked box—you will experience all manner of demons and devils let loose.

So then, should we avoid politics altogether? In 1 Timothy 2:1-3 Paul commands us to care, "First of all, then, I urge that supplications, prayers, intercessions, and thanksgivings be made for all people, for kings and all who are in high positions, that we may lead a peaceful and quiet life, godly and dignified in every way. This is good, and it is pleasing in the sight of God our Savior, who desires all people to be saved and to come to the knowledge of the truth." It really does matter who is leading our country, that is why Paul wants us to pray.

And in order to pray, you must care. Do you care enough to pray?

But if you are not careful in your caring, the demon named politics desires to possess you. It is rather easy for him to push you off the roof. The clearest way to tell if you have lost a balanced bearing is by asking yourself, "Do I care so much that I am beginning to hate those I disagree with? Do I view people across the aisle as villainous and vile? Have I grown so callous toward my political rivals that I don't even want them to know and experience the love of God?" It is natural and healthy to argue and debate ideas, in fact, it is necessary! But the moment you slander, demean and despise another human it is a sure sign that you care far too much.

I know this firsthand because I have fallen off the roof many a time. The Spirit of God will confront me in the quiet of night and ask me, "Chris, you think it is hard being a pastor of a relatively small church, try running a country?" He has shown me that I have actually hated people. When I see certain politician's faces on a television screen I instantly fume. This is not healthy. . . God forgive me! So if the president wants to go golfing again, who am I to begrudge him some downtime in the most pressure-filled job on earth?

We all are a part of this country, "We" are "the People." And as a Christian, it would do the U.S. of A. some good to have you and your God-given compassion for others involved in the decisions that are being made. If you disagree with that last statement, go live in Russia for a year and see what 70 years of atheism has wrought on the innocent. It is sad and devastating. I think the biggest problem with the downward slide of our country is that a whole bunch of godly Christians have simply given up. They left the discussion, their voices have been reduced to silence.

This reminds me of one more quote in "The Screwtape Letters" that I believe is germane to this discussion on politics and the lack of involvement of the good man:

"Indeed the safest road to Hell is the gradual one—the gentle slope, soft underfoot, without sudden turnings, without milestones, without signposts."

We can choose not to care hoping problems will all go away. We can hide away in our home, stay away from the polls, turn off the media and simply let it be. But it isn't that easy—God placed you in the world where we are to care about it. To love your neighbor. To help the needy, and elect people who create laws to be fair for all.

So, this political year, don't let the devil win and push you off the ridge of the roof. Stay steady, and pray. I know I need to begin there.

It's a Nurse Ratched World! (The Progressive's Obsession with Diagnosis)

Written March 23, 2016

"You hypocrite, first take the log out of your own eye, and then you will see clearly to take the speck out of your brother's eye." (**Matthew 7:5**)

The world has gone mad, and there are only a few adults left to run the asylum—and you my dear, misguided, blind friend, are definitely not one of them. So take your pills, sit there in your straight-jacket, and shut up. Nurse Ratched is in charge.

Who is Nurse Ratched? Those in this world who like to diagnose other people's problems and then tell them what to do and how to behave. People like the writer of a recent article in the Huffington Post I was asked to read last week; the title is "When You're Accustomed to Privilege, Equality Feels Like Oppression."

The author believes that there are those in our country that are like a guy at his work that will always take the right-of-way expecting people to move to the side when he walks by. When someone dares to bump into him he cries "foul." This, says the author, is how the privileged class in America behaves. If they don't always get their way, they whine and moan. So who is this whining privileged class according to this author? Listen to what he says:

All this anger we see from people screaming "All Lives Matter" in response to black protesters at rallies. All this anger we see from people insisting that their "religious freedom" is being infringed because a gay couple wants to get married. All these people angry about immigrants, angry about Muslims, angry about "Happy Holidays," angry about not being able to say bigoted things without being called a bigot...

The whining privileged class seems to be those who are simply trying to stand on traditional values and the rule of law. In many ways, I understand what he saying, and agree that we need to be accepting other people's opinions and not be "racist bigots." Yes, we live in a country that is democratic, so we need to listen and respect other people's ideas. But what if I disagree and really believe some things to be true and right? What if I am standing on real convictions and disagree with you on principle; does that make me a privileged jerk?

It seems like anyone who has any sort of standards, or believes that living morally is good for a community is the real villain; by creating guidelines for what we think promotes a civilized society, we are actually standing in the way of other's freedom. Not only are we not allowed to have a voice, but when we do express our position, those who disagree are given "carte' blanche" to attack and judge us. They are Nurse Ratched, we have become the inmate in the asylum:

"You are homophobic if you disagree with gay marriage, promoting trans-gendered bathrooms, and don't like the idea of a gay Boy Scouts."

"You are racist is you don't let a group of black protesters interrupt the political rally or demand for a waiting period for Muslims to have access into our country."

"You are a misogynist if you believe abortion is wrong, and want to stop funding an organization that may be trafficking human body parts."

"You are a selfish imperialist if you don't want to provide free health care, free education, free meals, free housing to the disadvantaged. You are a cold-hearted creep."

And Nurse Ratched is never wrong, she never has to clear the log out of her eye. Don't you see, what we once thought was "good" (teaching hard work, saving, sacrificing, encouraging marriage and family, rewarding a person because of character and not color) is now "bad." So we must now enforce Nurse Ratched's "new good": Which is to encourage everyone to "be and do" whatever they want to "be and do" while demanding others to pay for it. Those who complain about the "new good" need to take their pills, sit down and shut-up...and of course open their wallets.

I agree with Nurse Ratched that this world is messed up. But it is messed up on both sides. There are bigots on both sides, there are rich misers who hide under the establishment and tax codes written for their benefit on both sides, there are many who know how to play the system on both sides, and there are sexual perverts on both sides.

My problem with Nurse Ratched is that you are not allowed to argue with her, because <u>she alone</u> knows what is good for you!

Crime & Punishment in 2016

Written March 30, 2016

What is worse? 1. Having a boy who likes to dress like a girl demanding for the right to change in the girl's locker room, or 2. texting on your iPhone while walking down the street?

Seems like a no brainer, no one wants a locker room experimental free-for-all in a school full of hormone-charged teens. But not so fast...in our present nanny state with our new army of radical, foaming at the mouth progressive liberators, perversion is "in" and public responsibility and freedom is "out."

In the first case, some states are now being pressured by the ACLU to allow students to explore and live by their own chosen gender identity. As one article on MLive writes, "When it comes to bathroom access for transgender students, civil liberties groups say the law is clear: Students are entitled to use the restroom that aligns with their gender identity." It goes on to say, "The Michigan State Board of Education aims to make schools more welcoming to students who identify as lesbian, bisexual, gay, transgender or questioning. Among the recommendations: School staff address transgender students by their "chosen name," pronouns that "correspond to their gender identity," and allow students to use the restroom or locker room that's in accordance with their gender identity."

So if my daughter is showering after her soccer game in the locker room, Johnny is allowed to go in and dress in the same room if he feels like a girl for the day. Something is inherently wrong with that scenario. It is akin to having a gay Boy Scout leader sleeping in the same tent with your 10-year-old son. *It's not right, and you just know it!*

In case two, the state of New Jersey is now discussing the very real possibility that "distracted walking" is to be considered a crime where you can either be fined or receive jail time. What is categorized as distracted walking? Texting, internet surfing or selfie-taking while walking down the street. God forbid if you were to walk into a telephone pole while texting your BFF. Bumping smack into a street sign or innocent homeless man while he is panhandling on the corner of the street is not to be tolerated!

I ask you, "What is going on?" How are we to understand this "Brave New World" of American civility? I have two suggestions on how to make sense of this:

1. Traditional Standards of Morality are being systematically attacked and destroyed in America. God, guilt and shame are no longer allowed to hold sway over our desires and passions. In our world of fragile egos and overindulgence, the new sin is to make someone feel bad for their perversions, selfish inclinations and sinful lusts. God is the new villain; he wants to take away our fun and right to define our own identity. If I want to be a woman, I am going to be a woman, even if it is more than obvious God made me a man. So to "have it our way" we need to silence God and rip-up his repressive moral laws. Not only that, but our enlightened culture demands that "No one should ever regulate your right to end the life of a child in your womb, when to take your own life, or stop you from sleeping with whoever you want." We are the new masters of the Universe, regardless of whether it turns the Universe into an open sewer or not—"stand-down God"—we are in charge now!

58

2. But we all know if anything goes, innocent bystanders are bound to get hurt. So the liberal "Nanny State" has taken over, they now get to set down the new laws and rules because they will protect us, they always know better. Someone has to be in charge and progressive liberal politics and social re-engineering is now our new god. Progressives, like 2nd-grade elementary school teachers, think they know what is best for everyone and they have taken over the micromanagement of society through arbitrary law and enforced tolerance. Not only that, they love to control our personal freedoms as we behave publicly in the community. They watch over our speech, our dress, our gestures and now our texting. Hey, they got doctorates at the elite Ivy League schools so they are definitely smarter than your average mom, dad, construction worker and truck driver. And above all, they can never allow you to feel guilty before a Holy God, it may hurt your psyche.

The Prairie View A & M case:

If you don't believe me that justice these days is topsy-turvy I have the perfect case-study to prove my point. The African American female basketball coach at Prairie View A & M was recently fired because she had the gall to suspend two of her players after they decided to break team rules and date each other. She had issued a clearly written policy that stated, "Players may not have nonprofessional relationships with other players, coaches, managers trainers or any other persons affiliated" with the team. She said she enacted the rule after an assistant coach had a relationship with a player.

But the two players had filed a complaint alleging that their dismissal discriminated against them because of sexual orientation, and violated Title IX. Title IX is the federal law that bans sexual discrimination in any education program or activity receiving federal financial assistance.

Don't you see? The players felt discriminated against. Oh no, they might feel offended! We can't have that! But isn't the coach African American? And isn't she a woman? Yeah, but homosexuality trumps both of those. Personal sexual proclivities win these days. And plus the coach tried to enact "rules of conduct" which clearly are an archaic construct of our traditional authoritarian past, we no longer should be in slavery under such bondage.

The Book of Judges in the Bible is a story of chaos. It details the implosion of society and God's frustration with a wicked people. The way the book ends describes what was wrong with Israel, "In those days, there was no king in Israel. Everyone did what was right in his own eyes." (Judges 21:25)

America? Patriotism, the Military & Remembrance

Written June 3, 2016

I love America. I love our Flag. I love the history of our country: 1776, Fife & Drum Corps, old pictures of Presidents wearing white wigs, Williamsburg.

But is my love more a product of nostalgia founded on a memory of a small boy running in the back yard on a hot 4th of July night with a sparkler, than the reality of what is? I ask this because I am not sure if all Americans agree on what we mean by America?

Last week I received a few complaints from some patriotic parishioners that we didn't properly remember America in our church service. In what way should have we remembered it? Have all the veterans stand? We do that on Veteran's day. Memorial Day is meant to remember the dead—but you can't have those who died in wars past stand because they are already buried. Do we sing "God Bless America?" What if some patriotic Canadians are in the service or foreign exchange students from China and Germany? Are we claiming special favor when we ask God to bless American mountains and prairies? Will they be upset if we don't ask God to bless the Rhine River or Great Wall of Mao's China?

Is love of country wrong? There are a lot of things I am hating about our country right now. I will not ask God to bless our bathrooms, never. Men wearing women's dresses does not fall under my category of true Liberty. Nor am I going to sing about our abortion mills and selling of fetal tissue—that makes me sick! I guess some people don't think you can be an

American, or a real human for that matter, if you still are in your mother's womb?

Some people are sick of our greed and lack of compassion for the poor. Some others would say we give the poor far too much money with far too little accountability. America is a confusing, wonderful, disgusting and terrific place.

I think how I view America says more about me than what America actually is. My description of patriotism is more like a Rorschach inkblot test than an accurate accounting of life as it is from the Atlantic to the Pacific. What I see is usually what I want to see. Often those who want to sing songs about America at the church service see life through 1950's Norma Rockwell spectacles; whereas those who don't are wearing the much newer and more cynical Andy Warhol lenses.

In a strange way, this vast polarization of vision means America is really healthy. It infers that we are not yet expected to think monolithically like Nazis or Soviets or even the Khmer Rouge. We still have a free press, even though most of them have no problem lying to us. We still can assemble, even if some marches end in looting and riots. We still can own guns, even if the Chicago South Side is being riddled with blood and bullets every single day. We still have a choice.

There are so many questions left unanswered when it comes to America. There are so many different versions of what America is. Some people see it as the land of opportunity, others as a vast prison of exploitation. Some see it as the government of the people by the people for the people. Others see it as an elitists' social project protecting the marginalized and victimized minority where the word democracy has become nothing more than a badly told joke. Some see America as the last bastion of freedom in the world; others see it as a place where freedom has gone wild, along with its girls, gays and gorillas.

So, who and what is an American patriot? I don't know anymore.

I am proud that the Constitution is a Judeo-Christian product representing an accurate view of man's fallenness and the human heart's desire to control, however, I am ashamed of its dreadfully wrong anthropology. Black races were not considered fully human. To appease 18th-century slave-holders, the drafters of our freedom justified the legal bondage of so many. We can not ignore this sin! While others cannot move past it.

Yes, our military is the best in the world, but we are not always the most righteous. Are all soldiers to be considered heroes & saints? Or are some slackers joining the service just to receive a boatload of benefits and job opportunities from the government knowing they will not really face combat like our grandfathers used to? Do some soldiers just like to wear a uniform? Because it sure does feel good to be honored during patriotic parades. Do the women who fought for the right to go into combat really want to go into combat? Or is that too another political ploy for pushing this silly feminist equality narrative?

I love America, I really do. I just am not sure what America is? George Washington would blush to hear we recently had a President who had sex with an 18-year-old girl in his office; Jack Kennedy would probably have laughed about it. John Adams would turn in his grave to see us pass a thousand-page health-care reform bill without the majority of congressman knowing what is even in it; tricky Dick Nixon would applaud at how they got away with it. Joseph Goebbels would be jealous of our current day media's access to power and technological tools for mass manipulation.

After living in Russia for a year, traveling through Bulgaria, Germany, Poland, Austria, France, Israel and even Mexico I can say we as a country are truly blessed.

Democracy works, so does capitalism, so does private ownership, rule of law, and so does fair and just courts. But corruption still lingers in the shadows of every politician's heart. Lord Acton was right, power corrupts, absolute power corrupts absolutely. We aren't there yet. But we have started sliding toward Gomorrah.

If you love this country, help stop the slide. We need more than songs and nostalgic tears of what may have been to turn this country around. We need more than flags flying and trumpets blowing. We need more than soldiers marching and blowhards arguing. We need more than Facebook posting and Twitter sputtering. What we need is individual righteousness. We need people that will say no to corruption. We need people to serve others without needing applause or hero worship.

We need God. Fear him.

"Turn from evil and do good; seek peace and pursue it. The eyes of the LORD are on the righteous, and His ears are inclined to their cry. But the face of the LORD is against those who do evil, to sever their memory from the earth."

—Psalm 34:14-15

Are Gays Being Punished? No...We All Are!

Written June 13, 2016

"As long as idolatry exists in the world, God's fierce anger will exist in the world."
—Rabbi Rashi

This is the first time I have been asked to blog on a subject by more than four people in the span of a few hours. *"I was hoping you would have something to say about the shooting spree in Orlando?"* I didn't because I was still trying to make sense out of it, and I also was waiting for backlash against conservative communities of faith who hold to the position that homosexuality is biblically considered a sin. And I didn't want to voice my opinion in a culture who think people like me are to blame.

However, the first article I read this morning reported that the shooter's father believed and taught his son that, "God will punish those involved in homosexuality," saying it's, "not an issue that humans should deal with." In other words, those dancing at a gay bar deserve death by vigilante justice. We should show no pity, and shed no tears.

Really? Is that how we should respond to this murderous rampage?!? The worst in American history?

Many other questions came flooding to my mind: How do I feel about a gay bar being shot up? I am sure many people secretly believe "they had it coming to them?" How do I feel about 50 innocent people being gunned down? How, as a Christian community, are we to respond because I want to love the person but not affirm the sin?

I have four things to say to help give us some guidelines which hopefully will temper our opinions and allows us to voice them with reason instead of knee jerk reactions...

1. Jesus believes no one is innocent. (Luke 13:1-5)

When Jesus was alive two tragic events happened that were on the front page news, and they were also 'hot topics' of discussion for people living at that time. (1) A group of non-Jews went to the temple to worship God and Pontius Pilate had them murdered in cold blood. (2) A giant tower unexpectantly fell over and killed 18 people. Jesus' disciples wondered if all these people died because somehow they were worse sinners than the average person? Because surely, God only punishes wicked sinners, right?

So, in like fashion, I am sure many people are looking to Orlando saying, "the wicked sinners deserved it!"

Listen to Jesus' response:

"Do you think that these Galileans (Orlando gay bar customers) were worse sinners than all the other Galileans, because they suffered in this way? No, I tell you; but unless you repent, you will all likewise perish. Or those eighteen (50) on whom the tower in Siloam fell (who were gunned down) and killed them: do you think that they were worse offenders than all the others who lived in Jerusalem? No, I tell you; but unless you repent, you will all likewise perish."

Jesus is saying something devastating; there are no graded classes of sinners. We all are deserving the wrath of God (Romans 1:18). Ever since Adam sinned, wrath has been a constant shadow stalking us. Cancer, hatred, divorce, murder, lust, discord, adultery, and yes, homosexuality, are all results of a world under wrath. Wrath exists because this world of obstinate sinners (which includes you and me) does not want the righteous rule and help of God - so, he has let us have our way. Imagine leaving a daycare full of 3 year-olds alone for a week without adult supervision, sheer chaos. That is wrath, and we all deserve it because we all want a world without God. We have cast him aside, and now we must deal with it.

Death is coming soon to a theater near you: Maybe not by a terrorist's bullet, but it is coming, so "Repent!"

2. Jesus died for all sinners. (John 3:16)

What does this verse say? Who does God love? Everyone. Everyone. Including, believe it or not, the homosexual and the ISIS sympathizer. God loves them. And to win them to himself, he died for their sin. Read the Bible, especially Romans 5:6-11, and tell me, who is left out Christ's work on the cross.

No one. That is why...

3. Homosexuals need to hear about forgiveness, not more condemnation. (Luke 24:46-48)

Our job is to show pity, compassion, patience and kindness to everyone. We never can justify the mass killing of a group of people, even if we are not O.K. with their lifestyle choices. As Christians, we never support the shooting of liars, thieves, porn addicts, and the proud, do we? Remember, homosexuality is no different than your gluttony! And I could never imagine us wondering how to view people being shot in a McDonald's as we do this Orlando case.

We are to weep with those who weep. Remember, we should never rejoice at the murder of the "situationally" innocent. Morally, no one is innocent. But that doesn't mean they deserve to be shot down in cold blood either.

4. Extreme Islam is a religion of angry thugs.

If you don't believe me, read the Koran. Ask women how they live when Islam is given free rein like Iran, Saudi Arabia, Afghanistan and Pakistan? Their theology does not paint Allah as compassionate, he is known as "Capricious", meaning—he does what he does without remorse. Jehovah is a God of love, he sent his Son to die. Allah is a gangster. Islam is a curse.

And if you are a Muslim, ask yourself two things: What do your scriptures teach about infidels? (this includes Jews, Christians and Unbelievers) If Islam is a religion of peace, why don't you do all you can to rid this world of terrorism? Christians are quick to disavow our radicals: We stand up and condemn churches like Westboro Baptist, they are a complete embarrassment to us. Are you equally embarrassed and full of rage concerning your Muslim brothers who kill? Then say something!!!!

"Yeah, but wasn't Muhammed Ali a man of peace?" You don't really know Muhammed Ali if you believe that.

A final word:

Are guns the cause? That is for "the people" and politicians to battle about, but we must admit high capacity machine guns do increase the potential to fuel more serial slayings. Like alcohol and date rape - rape is the sin, alcohol lubricates the lust that causes it.

So, think! Don't react. Love people, show compassion for the dead. And repent from your sin before you judge another person. Jesus said, "first take the log out of your eye!" (Luke 6:41).

Popular
Culture

MONKEYS IN THE CIRCUS

"The battle line between good and evil runs through the heart of every man."

—Aleksander Solzhenitsyn

The human animal is fascinating, I could watch them forever. Not one of them is the same. Two eyes, two ears, one nose and one mouth and still they fascinate. Today we live in a world that tries to homogenize people by groups, but you can't, people are people. As Jim Morrison once said, "People are strange."

I know myself and I still don't understand me.

This section is for the purpose of studying the fantastic beast called man. And when I say man, I mean it in a general sense. So if you are a woman you are still a man. And if you are offended by being called a man it is your own fault because I am not intending to offend. In fact, if you are a woman you are more unique than just being clumped into a category called woman...I am a man but more than a man.

I am a Shapka wearing man. And people who wear Shapkas already are already embarrassing themselves, so if they offend, they just cant help it!

So consider this section like a version of the Twilight Zone where humans land on a planet and they find themselves being locked in cages, they want out, but they can't, because they landed in a zoo!

Yes, we are living in God's zoo!

Vampire Make-Over

Written January 28, 2014

Vampires, very, very dangerous!

At least that I what I grew up believing as a kid. I learned while watching the Night Stalker on TV, vampires often roamed the dark shadows of city streets driven by thirst, "Va-a-a-anting to suck my blood." From Bela Lugosi to the suburban creeper on "Fright Night," I convinced myself never to trust a white-faced, sharp-toothed Count from Transylvania.

But my contempt for vampires was soon to be challenged; my wife brought home a rather innocent looking book with an apple on the front. "What book is that?" She replied, "It is called Twilight, it is about a gorgeous vampire named Edward. He's so dreamy!" (She didn't quite say it like that, but that is what she meant). I was appalled. "You mean to tell me, you...like...vampires??"

She went on to explain how vampires are now COOL. Edward and his family only suck the blood of animals, and they are friends to humans. He even is in love with a human girl named Bella because he is intoxicated with the scent of her blood and wants to be her eternal soul-mate. "How romantic!" Well, as most of us know, the Twilight series hit the big-time in book sales & silver screen, and vampire mania went crazy. Now vampires are all the rage, lovable fuzz balls now for us to eagerly embrace; the perfect model of what fathers everywhere hope their daughters would marry. The American people took the monster and domesticated him. A vampire has now become a hero...hence, the vampire makeover.

A few years ago one of the students in my youth group pulled me aside and sheepishly said, "I am really having a problem with my mom." After a few seconds of silence, I asked her **for** more specifics. Here is what she said, "Well, the best way to put it is that my mom...well...she is like a vampire. She is one person in daylight, putting on a great show as a responsible mother for all to see; and then when night comes she completely changes. She drags me with her to all the seedy bars & clubs while she tries to be a sensual lady trying to pick up other women. I am supposed to respect her new lifestyle choices, but how can I when she has turned into an irresponsible adolescent driven by lust?" Like a vampire lurking & thirsting in the shadows...

Well, most American experts, teachers, and cultural connoisseurs tell us now not to worry, lust is now a good thing. Sexual preferences now define who people are, they can't help being thirsty. The contempt we once had for sensual obsessions and perversions has been domesticated; instead of encouraging self-control, it has now become a repressive vice. Self-expression and personal freedom is the moral high ground to claim and fight for...the vampire is now our hero. And God?

Well...he is now society's primary villain. "Why do you bring charges against me? You have all rebelled against me," declares the Lord. (Jeremiah 2:29)

75

Hatin' Jessie's Girl

Written February 6, 2014

I was in a dark state of mind: it was last Monday, my day off, I am a pastor, I do that! It was a depressing Monday, early February, snow was falling again, it was bone cold.

As I meditated on my past sermon, reflected on important personal conversations and nursed a Super Bowl hangover (not from beer, but from Doritos & pop), my wife and I pulled into Arby's to get an early lunch. While unwrapping a hot roast beef, a song came over the speakers: I knew it instantly with its cheesy guitar riff, yep, it was Rick Springfield's "Jessie's Girl." It is the kinda song where the melody and lyrics make me want to pull out my hair:

You know I wish that I had Jessie's girl

I wish that I had Jessie's girl

Where can I find her, a woman like that?

It is the perfect stalker song. An ode to unrequited love, a sappy melancholy man wishing he could have another guys girl, "I wish that I could have...I wish that I could, could..." ENOUGH ALREADY! And then my dark mind started thinking; I wish that I had the money Rick Springfield earned for writing such a worthless song. I wish that I had money for all the worthless songs that have made it big (I was thinking of artists like Jay Z, Katie Perry, Lady Gaga...I wish that I had...) My dark thoughts plunged deeper; I wish I didn't have to struggle so much preaching while worthlessness rules on a global scale, schleps of every size and shape raking in millions. How does someone like Kim Kardashian make millions? Ah-h-h-h....I could scream!

I told you, dark thoughts on a cold Monday.

While finishing my sandwich, licking Arby's sauce drippings from my thumb, I had one more thought, "My only hope is heaven, all chips in." If there was no heaven I would lose my mind. Springfield's net worth is $12 million dollars, bad 80's hair and all, for cryin' out loud, where is the justice? "I wish..." But wait, sanity returned, The words of another song filled my mind, Psalm 73:15-20:

When I tried to understand all this, it troubled me deeply till I entered the sanctuary of God; then I understood their final destiny. Surely you place them on slippery ground; you cast them down to ruin. How suddenly are they destroyed, completely swept away by terrors! They are like a dream when one awakes; when you arise, Lord, you will despise them as fantasies.

We pull out of the Arby's parking lot and turn on the radio. It's James Blunt, "My life is brilliant, my love is pure, I saw an angel, of this I'm sure..." Oh no, not another melancholy sappy stalker...turn it off! But, "I wish that I..." No Chris, no! A thousand times NO!

You have got it made, as Psalm 73 ends…

Whom have I in heaven but you? And earth has nothing I desire besides you. My flesh and my heart may fail, but God is the strength of my heart and my portion forever.

"Hey Look! It's Brad Pitt & Miley Cyrus!"

Written February 6, 2014

Wisdom cries aloud in the street,
in the markets she raises her voice;
at the head of the noisy streets she cries out;
at the entrance of the city gates she speaks:
"How long, O simple ones, will you love being simple?"

(Prov. 1:20-22)

Great question: "How long, O simple ones?" I think the appropriate answer to that last question is, "For a very, very, very long time." That is why I cast some tasty bait into the cyber sea, two celebrity names that I know are always trending, thrown out like minnows for the simple ones to bite on to. I am testing a theory..."I believe American homes & culture are raising simpletons 25 times the rate as the production of the wise." To prove it, I picked two of the top media darlings just to see how many hits I get on my Blog. (I was going to put Rebecca Black out there too, but I just couldn't stomach it and I don't want to get hate mail). I know it is wrong to go fishing for numskulls, but I am trying to prove a point.

Deep down I want people to read my blog, that is one of the reasons I write it. If people don't come to read, I figure then maybe I need to either write better & deeper, display a little bit of more insight, or consider picking up another hobby to better myself, like playing Parcheesi with my youngest daughter. I have only been doing this for two months and I want to get better. So as I mentally wrestled with how to improve, I decided to check which posts in the past two months got the most hits so I can find out what it is that brings people in to read. Well, I found something that saddened me (I should have seen it coming):

There is a direct correlation between number of hits on a post and silliness.

And the more biblical and serious the subject, the more people stay away. Far and away the most read post on my blog, in just two months time, is the one about the song "Jesse's Girl." I don't think people hit on it for the possible intriguing & heartfelt discussion as much as we are drawn to the banality of pop culture. So that is why I threw Brad and Miley out there. I want to see how easy it is to catch some foolish fish.

So, you may be wondering at this point in the blog, "If I am reading this then that means Chris is calling me a fool?" No, I am simply wondering why we are drawn so easily to things that are so silly? Why do we care about things that are eternally so insignificant that we will spend most of our lives using our brain cells thinking, talking and browsing to look for more of this trash? I ask it to myself, "How long Oh simple Chris will you love being simple?"

Even Alec Baldwin, a frivolous celebrity in his own right, is beginning to ask these same questions toward the media where he once took center stage in. In his farewell piece in the recent New York Magazine, he has decided to stop being a public celebrity because it is killing his life, "They want clicks, I get it. They've gotta have clicks for their advertisers, so they're going to need as much Kim Kardashian and wardrobe malfunctions as possible." He hits it right on the head. — we want clicks, traffic, tweets, friends — and the quickest and easiest way to do that is to dumb down! The

"Tonight Show" has figured this out, more silly SNL skits with Fallon and the less talk and discussion, the better. It gets more hits.

Christians, can't we do better? Aren't we supposed to think? (Romans 12:1)

I know, I know, you would love to talk about it, but something is pressing at the moment. You are going to have a date night tonight with your spouse and you need to check theater times: THE LEGO MOVIE IS HERE! YAHOOO!

God & Green Beer (St. Patrick's Edition)

Written March 14, 2014

Satan knows something we often forget—idolatry starts in the mind.

So he will imprint onto your mind false images of God, and there are two main ones he has people walking a tight-rope between. On one side he wants us believing that God is hard-hearted, mean & nasty: He is not for you! In Matthew 25:24 Jesus tells a parable about a man who hid his one talent in the ground, and when the master came by and asked him why, he said, "I knew you were a hard & stern man." This is the view of God the nuns in my elementary school had me believing. Last week in my sermon, I said how as a kid I thought the purpose of church was to be 'Miserable.' And when you think God wants you miserable, Satan grins with pleasure. (Because he wants you to not want to be with God.)

But as we saw in Jesus' first miracle last week, this view of God is categorically untrue. He made wine out of water, he joined in a marriage celebration, and he provided needy people with more than they could "ask for or imagine." Hopefully, last week's message completely destroyed that first lie in your mind? But Satan is crafty, if he can't get you one way, he will push you completely the other way. The other side of the tight-rope is to convince you that God is a wimp: He is naïve, soft & impotent (meaning he is an old man that won't lift a finger against our will and desires, "Ah, go ahead sonny, do whatever you want!"). Psalm 10:11-13 describes this view plainly for us: "God has forgotten; he covers his face and never sees."

Personally speaking, I walked this tight-rope: As I grew older I outgrew the nuns' threats of doom; and slowly without ever realizing it, my friends became the main influence on how I thought about God. Instead of associating God with Sister Joan of Arc's ruler; my new image of God was a raised glass of green beer.

This wasn't brought to my attention until my senior year in college during St. Patrick 's Day Weekend. In almost every student's mind, from Thursday afternoon to Saturday Night, it was your obligation to skip class so you could participate in the plethora of St. Patrick Day parties around campus. "Green Beer was everywhere: a 20 kegger on Thursday, a 50 kegger Friday, a 25 kegger on Saturday." If you ever wondered where the makers of the "Walking Dead" TV series got their idea, I wouldn't be surprised if one of the writers visited my college on that St. Patrick's Day weekend.

Needless to say, Sunday morning was awfully quiet around campus as people slept off their weekend of a "hops & barley headache." I can remember feeling compelled to go to church on Sunday at the campus chapel. Noon starting time allowed enough leeway for those who wanted to cover their guilt and shame to make it out of bed and arrive for mass. I was surprised because it was relatively full; as the half-awake students sat in their padded pews I will never forget what the priest said, "I know most of you are in no condition to really pay much attention so I will say a quick prayer and let you go home early." As I looked around the chapel, students were smiling and murmuring to one another, "What a cool priest! Man, this is great, he really gets us." As people filed out, I just sat there because one word haunted my mind: Hypocrite!

We all like nice Jesus—but is that who Jesus really is? 2 Corinthians 11:4 hints at the idea that many false teachers use Jesus' name, but it may not be the Jesus who actually exists (mental idolatry). The Jesus the Bible describes is dangerous: He drove people out of the temple when they were using God's house to make a profit. He yelled at Peter and called him "Satan" when Peter didn't want him to go to the cross and die. Jesus is coming again to earth in blazing fire flanked by his army of powerful angels (2 Thessalonians 1:6-10). And...Jesus is Holy.

With that being said, we also should be holy. In 1 Corinthians 15:32 Paul was hypothetically speculating on what our human response should be if Jesus actually never rose from the dead. One of his answers was to "Eat Up and Drink Hearty because we are all Doomed to Die" But Paul's whole point of chapter 15 was to persuasively argue that "Jesus did Rise from the Dead;" therefore we must live differently. He puts it like this in verses 33-34: "Do not be misled; Bad company corrupts good character. Come back to your senses as you ought, and stop sinning; for there are some who are ignorant of God - I say this to your shame."

One last question: When Jesus made a whip out of cords, was he just foolin' around?

Counterfeit Grit (Defining True Strength)

Written March 24, 2014

Don't cry for me, but I wouldn't mind a little sympathy—I had it terribly hard growing up because I always had to walk to school. From elementary school to high school, I had to hoof it; in sleet, snow, wind, rain, and being from Cleveland I rarely walked in sunshine. Instead of walking, it sure would have been nice to have my very own vehicle to come tooling into the high school parking lot with. I also attended a very wealthy school which made it extra hard to walk. It seemed like every student but me was given their own car once they got their drivers license. I can vividly remember one student who got a "Suped-Up" Ford pick-up truck from his rich daddy... man was it nice. I remember it well because the first day he had the truck he came flying into the parking lot squealing the tires, revving his engine and blasting Metallica. I thought to myself, *"Now whoever this is, he has to be one tough dude."*

As the truck came to a halt, students gathered around, and to everyone's surprise, out jumped one of the skinniest and shortest kids in the school. You sure can't judge a book by its cover! Not only that, but this single experience became a watershed moment in my understanding of the world. I realized, "Just because a person could push their foot down hard on a gas pedal and can turn on a radio loud doesn't make that person tough and gritty." I had that same kid in gym class and he would be the first one to whine & complain if we ever had to run, lift weights, or put on boxing gloves. That truck, the loud engine, was all show! I call this "Counterfeit Grit."

Over the years I have learned this principle also applies when it comes to determining someone's moral strength, courage and grit as well. I have found that those who are lacking in it often hide behind loud & harsh words, threats, snap judgments, and demands for serious punishment. The problem with the counterfeit is that we believe it to be the "real thing." I have seen time and time again where the loudest mouths and harshest words get to make most of the decisions, and usually, it ends up resulting in everyone's detriment. But as they say, the best way to recognize a counterfeit is to first learn what the "Genuine Article" looks like.

The "Genuine Article" of true strength & grit is, of course, Jesus of Nazareth. And I believe the most profound example of his grit is found in 1 Peter 2:19-24—I THINK YOU WILL BE SURPRISED:

"For this is a gracious thing, when, mindful of God, one endures sorrows while suffering unjustly. For what credit is it if, when you sin and are beaten for it, you endure? But if when you do good and suffer for it you endure, this is a gracious thing in the sight of God. For to this you have been called, because Christ also suffered for you, leaving you an example, so that you might follow in his steps. He committed no sin, neither was deceit found in his mouth. When he was reviled, he did not retaliate in return; when he suffered, he did not threaten, but continued entrusting himself to him who judges justly. He himself bore our sins in his body on the tree, that we might die to sin and live to righteousness. By his wounds you have been healed."

I just want to point out two things, that's it:

1. HE DID NOT RETALIATE: Stop and think about that for one second, this should blow your mind! First, take into account that Jesus made the world, he was perfect and yet the people he created, "Spit on him, punched him, mocked him,

ignored him, laughed at him, and hung him on a cross." And he did not retaliate! Counterfeits retaliate, usually loudly like a skinny guy stomping on a gas pedal—it takes nothing to do it. But to be patient under injustice and let God work, now that takes courageous faith! And tell me, you who live in America, do you really have it that bad? Seriously? Is your situation so tough that it seems God has treated you unfairly?

2. HIS WOUNDS BROUGHT HEALING: His willingness to wait gave the world the opportunity to change and be healed. If Jesus got fed up, and vented his anger immediately, demanding punishment "Now!" you and I would be toast. Is it easy to wait for someone to change while you bear up under their faults and mistakes? No, it takes real strength, courage and grit to do that! Think about raising your kids: when they were babies they often kept you up a night crying and whining. Why didn't you retaliate by yelling at them and demanding them to change or you were going to put them up for adoption? Love, right!

Love sees future potential—not the present failure. Love hopes for God's spirit to transform hearts. Love hopes for God's Spirit to transform hearts. Love keeps no record of wrongs because it entrusts itself to "him who judges justly!" This is why James 2:13 says, "Mercy triumphs over Judgment." Showing people "Mercy" may cost you more, it will demand of you courage and grit, but when you let it accomplish its work there is the grand possibility for a transformed human being...a trophy of God's grace to be displayed!

All "judgment" can do is judge, that's easy and quick, but it shuts the door for hope and mercy to do its work! Like squealing your tires in a parking lot—it seems cool but it sure ruins your tread!

Personality Testing: "I still haven't found what I am looking for....knowing myself"

Written February 24, 2016

Last night I took a personality test at 16personalities.com
After responding to 100 questions, this test promised to reveal to me my true self. I was shocked by the results. It said that I was an "Entertainer": I have to be the life of every party, I don't like to talk about the big issues of life, and I am only looking for fun. I never knew this is who I am? In some ways, I feel more complete knowing this.

This morning I was reading an article that stated how Bernie Sanders, the white-haired, Jersey talking democratic candidate made this statement, "Most Republicans and conservatives are naturally racist, greedy and lacking compassion to those who are stuck in poverty." Uh oh, for most of my life I have voted Republican and looked for the most conservative candidates on the ballot. Does that mean...it must mean...I am a cold-hearted hater!

The other day I heard the rantings of a very well known feminist talking about most men over the age of 40 in our country: "they are selfish, controlling and lust driven." I am a man over 40, I am ashamed of myself.

A year ago, my daughter, had me take a "Divergent Test" based on the best selling movie of the same name. It said I am both "Dauntless and Abnegation." This means I don't care while caring too much. Who am I?

I was reading a history book explaining how the German warlike spirit is what caused most of the major wars. I have mostly German blood flowing through my veins. I got it from my mom who eats sour kraut for fun. It went on to say that "although Germans were very industrious and efficient, they also were calculating and cruel." I feel terrible about this.

I took a Lord of the Rings test two years ago that said I was an Orc. That is all it said...what does that mean? I like to eat Hobbit flesh and drink the blood of squirrels? How did they know?

I was watching a debate between an evangelical apologist and an atheist. The atheist made a statement that most Christians are disillusioned and gullible saps. I am not just a Christian, but I sell it to others on a daily basis. What does that make me...a peddler of false promises and illusions? What manner of wretch am I?

I am a Midwesterner as well, as compared to those from the South and West I am less hospitable, more to myself and by nature a rather boring family man. According to that list, I wouldn't want to hang out with me.

I also am an American. You know what that means! I am an Imperialist that enjoys living off the backs of the third world poor who work in sweatshops and dwell in shanty-towns. Why am I so indifferent to the plight of others?

The most insightful article yet was from a psychology journal that showed how the youngest child in the family, which I am, is a people pleaser and family clown.

I am not sure if I even know myself anymore; and worse than that, I don't like who I am. If I could I would run away from myself. I can't. So what are my options? Let the social experts and political hacks define me? Take a test and submit to its results? Just obey the commands of my German, male chauvinist self?

I choose death.

"I have been crucified with Christ. It is no longer I who live, but Christ who lives in me. And the life I now live in the flesh I live by faith in the Son of God, who loved me and gave himself for me."

—*Galatians 2:20*

Can a Woman be a Villain?

Written June 8, 2016

"Hortensio, though her father be very rich, any man is so
very a fool to be married to hell?"
—*Taming of the Shrew*

When it comes to our obsessive tendency to assign blame when things in the world go haywire, doesn't it seem like men always get the shaft? Are we too soft toward women? Should we place some of the responsibility of our problems at the feet of the femme fatales of the world—those evil women who seduce poor naive saps and lead them to their destruction and the rest of the world with it? (Proverbs 5:1-5)

2 weeks ago, I wrote a blog that received a number of comments. One of which seemed to think I was harping on men while giving women of the world a pass. As I looked back on what I wrote, I think the comments were accurate. I did only point out the selfish behavior of the men of our society while letting women off the hook. I did paint men as irresponsible adolescents. Silly little boys not willing to grow up; fools, fops, nitwits and buffoons.

And you know what...I will not retract my writings. Men are to blame. Men are the problem. Men are the fools. And since I am a male, I also am included in this indictment.

Oh, I know, some of you men out there vehemently disagree, you are up in arms when every television show paints the dad as the dummy, or the straight guy as the loudmouth jerk, or the white man as the bigoted dolt. But tell me, when was the last time you told a woman how you really felt? When is the last time you stood up to your wife and disagreed with her, or have you been reduced to silence because you don't want to hurt her feelings? Is that her fault or yours?

Do you complain or stay quiet when your wife takes another selfie, posts on Instagram her latest low-calorie meal, or spends 4 hours on her iPhone looking at what different things she can do with a mason jar on Pinterest? Do you keep buying closets full of princess dresses and dolls and Frozen paraphernalia because your little girl blinks her big brown eyes? That lack of self-control is on you bro!

When was the last time you had the guts to tell your 18 year old daughter considering the military that she isn't as strong as 90% of the boys in her grade, or pointed out how silly it is when women try to prove they can be just as intimidating on the front lines in combat as the men in her platoon? (See the silly comments by the winner of the Miss U.S.A. Beauty Pageant). You won't say those things because you don't want to be labeled as a chauvinist.

Is that the woman's fault or yours? You are scared to tell the truth. You are afraid to point out that Hilary is only able to make it as a candidate because she is a woman. It is your fault for letting your wife's emotions make you cancel your plans to go camping with your son so you help her do laundry on Saturday. Don't blame women, blame yourself. Eve may have eaten the apple first, but God still blamed Adam...he didn't have the guts to tell her no.

Why do so many of our daughters swoon for Justin Bieber? Milk toast dads let them. Why are boys overweight and lazy? Dads don't push them. See, men are to blame. I would even say feminism is mostly a reaction against absent fathers and selfish tyrannical dads. I will take it one step farther—I believe homosexuality often is born from the lack of male attention when boys are growing up (or a perverted uncle who has been left unchecked out in the barn). Again, it is the man's fault.

You want to stop date rape? Dads need to teach daughters that drinking parties are not wise choices because they are infested with brutal drunk men who are not there simply for deep conversation. They also need to tell their daughters that wearing barely any clothing to a party is not smart, it just isn't. If a daughter is drawn to drunken men it often is a tell-tale sign that the dad they know is probably a lust driven fool himself?

Fathers have the sole responsibility to teach sons that drunkenness is not manly and treating drunk women as their helpless prey is Satanic, it is the height of wickedness, and it is the poison of a twisted shrunken soul. Frat boy foolishness is often the outgrowth of fatherly failure.

Don't you see? It all starts from men. God first loved us...so likewise, dads should follow suit, and love, love, love.

I am by no means downplaying the role of moms...but I do think moms are dying for a man to follow. The only reason a feminist will resist that last statement is because they have never been led by a truly loving man. I feel sorry for feminists, transgenders, orphans and casualties of divorce— the greatest gift a child could receive is to be under the training and protection of a fierce man who fully loves you (and we need to not let women like Beyoncé ruin the word 'fierce", she isn't fierce, she is insecure).

All of this feminist and progressive angst and anger against men is born from an unfulfilled longing, the hope of having a godly father deferred.

So can a woman be a villain? Sure, but mature men can handle it. Confident men are not threatened or worried—they have nothing to prove. My dad loved baiting my sister. While at the dinner table he would look at me and say, "Chris, you need to cut the lawn, and remember, only us men can handle the hard work so you better do a good job." My sister Steph would stand up, and say, "I can do anything Chris can do! I am not a weak girl!" So she would run out the front door and the next thing I know she would be revving up the mower and for the next two hours, she would be out cutting the lawn.

My dad would look at me and say, "See, it works every time." He loved my sister, and she loved him, but somehow our world made her feel like she needed to compete to be someone of worth. She didn't. We were best friends, and after she was done cutting the lawn my dad would compliment her on her good work. Often remarking, "Steph, you know I was just kidding. I know you can do it, and don't let any man tell you different."

I think the real villain is the woman who is duped; the one who really believes she needs to compete to be complete. I always wonder, "Did she ever feel loved by her dad?" Probably not.

See, men really are to blame.

A Boy, A Marble & A Bathtub

Written June 24, 2016

"Christians have won an insufferable reputation for always dispensing answers, even when no one has a question."
—Os Guinness

How would you like to raise six wild kids, all born in an eight year span, while your husband was a traveling salesman gone most of the week traversing the continental United States? You would have to be one tough cookie to do it.

Well, my mom was one tough cookie!

She was raised to be tough: Daughter of two German farmers who moved to a working-class neighborhood in Dayton, Ohio. Her mom was a waitress at a bar while her dad worked in a factory. My mom had to take the public bus to school and landed a job as a secretary immediately out of High School. She pretty much raised herself. So you could say, she grew up in the tough German school of hard knocks.

Needless to say, raising six kids for her was a piece of cake. I was the easiest one of those kids, I was also the youngest, the baby boy. My sisters still claim I was her favorite. Why shouldn't I be? I was the cutest, the happiest, the smartest and most peace-loving. I was the most humble too!

So with a barrel-full of kids scampering around the house, she would be busy cleaning, cooking and watching "As The World Turns". She also would rarely answer the front door when people came calling. If she wasn't expecting a friend over, it was her habit to ignore the "Ding-Dong" of our loud, annoying doorbell. She told us not to answer it if it was a stranger; because more than likely it was one of the irritating Encyclopedia pushers, or Kirby vacuum cleaner sales nuts— and she didn't have the time or patience to listen to some lousy sales pitch.

For all intents and purposes, the Weeks' front door was considered "Closed for Business" to all unwanted visitors during the day. My German mom had better things to do.

That is until that fateful day when the whole Treemont Fire Department came knocking in earnest on our front door...seven strangers outfitted in full fire gear, knock, knock, knocking on our front door—a group my mom was more than willing and ready to open the front door, back door and second floor window to. Here is what happened:

We lived in a beautiful English Tudor home nestled nicely in the middle of a quiet suburb of Columbus, Ohio called Upper Arlington. On this particular day, all six of the Weeks kids were scattered around the house playing games, running in the backyard or watching "Captain Kangaroo" on the television set. I was bouncing around the house as a four-year-old, doing things a four-year-old does.

And then I had to go to the bathroom. I slogged up the stairs to the second-floor bathroom, closed the door, and locked it. The oak doors of our house were well made, and they also had a solid locking system that took a double turn of the bolt to secure it. I sat on the toilet, did my business, and then got ready to go back downstairs to do some more four-year-old things. I think I even washed my hands this time?

But when I tried to open the door to leave, it wouldn't budge. It was locked—and I forgot how to unlock it. I may have been a cute little guy, but I wasn't yet the brilliant problem solver that I am now. I was only four, give me a break! Anyhow, after many attempts, I started pounding, screaming and crying,

"Mom, I am stuck! Mom, I am locked in! Mom, I am going to die! Mom, H-E-L-P !"

Did I mention, I was also a bit dramatic? My mom came running and tried to open the door from the outside. It wouldn't budge. There was no way to unlock it from the outside. Talk about security, they sure did know how to make a door back in the day. Being a good non-emotional German, she was calm under pressure...but I wasn't, I had a lot of my dad's Italian/Polish passion. "Mom, get me out of here!"

She tried to explain to me how to turn the bolt, but it still wouldn't move. And plus it was hard to see through my stream of hot tears. I tried and cried, tried and cried. Nothing. My sisters even came up to help calm me through the door. But to no avail—I was an inconsolable wreck.

This went on for a good hour. But the door remained closed, and I remained trapped in the upstairs bathroom alone. Poor little desperate guy...it still breaks my heart thinking about it.

A brilliant idea popped into my mom's head, "I will call the fire department, they will know what to do." After she made the call, in mere minutes you could hear the wailing & whirring of the fire truck siren come screaming down the street, "YEee YEee YEee-HOOONNK, HOOONNNK!" The whole department came to the rescue for a four-year-old boy trapped.

While one team knocked on each entrance, front door, back door, side door; another team got out a giant ladder and extended it to the second-floor window. They all were outfitted with both axe and helmet. One brave firefighter climbed the ladder, and when he reached the window, luckily it was unlatched and he opened it with ease. He jumped through the window with extreme bravery.

In the flash of a quick second, he found me. There I was, calmly playing marbles in our old porcelain bathtub.

I guess I found something to do that a four-year-old loves to do, play with marbles in the bathtub—I forgot all about my terrible, horrible predicament. I looked up at the fireman and said, "Hi, want to play marbles?"

The deft firefighter walked over to the door, and with the quick flip of the lock, it sprung open and my worried mom ran in to get her son with relief and gratitude. My sisters all laughed at me with cynical unbelief, "We were worried sick, and you are playing marbles? Figures!!!" All was well!

Do you realize, you can't open the front door until people behind it are desperate? Do you realize the gospel can't enter into a heart until that heart is asking for it?

Os Guinness in his book on Apologetics writes this, "...in our age most people are untroubled rather than unreached, unconcerned rather than unconvinced, and they need questions as much as answers - or questions that raise questions that require answers that prompt people to become genuine seekers." Pascal said in his 'Pensees' one of the main tasks of the Christian teacher is, "to arouse in man the desire to find truth."

My German mom kept her front door closed to the knocking of the outside entreaties of the public, that is, until her little boy was trapped and she needed help. And then, because of her personal unsolvable dilemma, she was more than willing to open the door to those who had the answers she needed.

As enlightened Christians, we do have the answers, but no one is asking because they think they are doing just fine. Our job in this smug age of luxury and distraction is not to prove we have the right answers as much as to awaken people to their internal desperation. Everyone needs Jesus, they just don't know it. But when crisis comes calling, people will be hungry for God's peace; and they will find in the gospel a boy playing marbles in the bathtub. The soft and kind grace of God has always been there waiting. Most people are just too closed to it to appreciate it!

Ironically, people are in need of a real crisis to bring them to God's peace. And until the crisis comes, the doorbell will never be answered. Your job, my Christian friend, is to arouse desire and desperation in the hearts of those around you, and until then, all doors will be as solidly locked as a second-floor bathroom door was for my mom.

A boy, a marble and a bathtub. I never knew my silly four-year-old ways could open up such windows of wisdom? I guess sometimes it takes 47 years to see it?

Beyond Tom Petty (Why Do I Blog?)

Written June 27, 2016

Don't come around here no more
Don't come around here no more
Whatever you're looking for
Hey! don't come around here no more
I've given up, I've given up
I've given up on waiting any longer

—Tom Petty, "Don't Come Around Here No More"

There has to be more than this?

This question welled up in my soul out of nowhere and set me on a search for "real" meaning—that to this day, I am in constant pursuit of. I just can't stop, and quite frankly, that is why I blog, preach, read and wonder. As Socrates once quipped, "An unexamined life is not worth living." That is why it puzzles me why people are so easily satisfied with banal, trivial, and fleeting things. Unexamination is our cultural epidemic.

But who am I to talk? For the first 23 years of my life, I was, as C. S. Lewis wrote, "far too easily pleased" with the mud pies I was making and enjoying. That is until I saw Tom Petty in concert, where something was set aflame in my heart. It is not to be satisfied, now I search...

The year was 1985 and he just released the album "Southern Accents" which was enormously popular; especially with my friends who liked his quirky and odd musical style. Many people call his music "stoner rock". I was asked to accompany four of my friends to see him in concert, and we were all really jazzed up to see him (cool 80's lingo). The concert was in my hometown of Cleveland, and we made a night of it. I really don't remember who opened, or who I was with, but I do remember when Tom Petty first walked on stage. The crowd went crazy when all of his 130 pound skinny, scraggly-haired, bony-kneed frame came shuffling out on stage.

All eyes were fixed on this singular gaunt man. And then it happened, the moment I will never forget, the moment that has been haunting me and causing me to question all the things we, as a society, accept as true, real, popular, and praiseworthy. Tom Petty, with guitar strapped to his side, approached the microphone, and grabbing it with both hands, looked out on all of us and said, "Hello Cleveland!" The place erupted, people went berserk, and my friend next to me said this, "Can you believe it? He said Cleveland? He actually said Cleveland!"

Right at that moment, everything went into slow motion: I looked around and watched all these people willing to bow in worship to a skinny, skeletal man because he knew the name of the city he was performing in. I don't know how to describe it to you, but it felt like the very pores and fabric of existence expected, no, demanded of me to join in the adoration as well. No questions were to be asked, I was to offer myself in total submission, with all of my senses and reason, to the worship of someone who simply knew what was patently obvious to us all, "We were in Cleveland...Yes, a five-year-old could figure that out." But it was more than this, I felt like a tiny fish caught in a giant school of ignoramuses swimming to our certain death because both the cultural current and our human blindness was flowing and forcing all of us that way.

I wanted out. I wanted to breathe. I wanted reason. I wanted to be a thinking man.

As you read this, you may be thinking that going to a concert and applauding a great musician may not seem like a life-altering experience. But it was for me. I was pushed out, forced to look at everything anew. In that moment of time, I was tired of being, as Pink Floyd says, a cog in the machine. And that machine was not, as we are fooled to believe, the vast imperial, economic, monster of American greed and finance. The machine for me was this crowd of blind, amoral, independent and ignorant humanity.

We all claim independence, and yet we all clap for a silly man who can say Cleveland. I started noticing this everywhere. People all think the same, react the same, get tattoos the same way, vote the same, get angry the same, watch movies the same, drink the same, look at porn the same...while we are all made to believe we are unique and special. All rebels, when in fact, when we are nothing more than reactionary robots.

I wanted more. I wanted that for which I have been designed. And I still am searching for.

That is primarily why I blog. People ask me, "Blogging on a consistent basis takes a lot of work. Why do you do it? People will get mad at you and you don't need the headache?" I do it for three reasons:

1. **REFINE** both my thinking and understanding. I was told if you ever really want to be a better thinker, writer, communicator you need to go public. This is where you will be challenged. This is where your worldview will be tested. Anyone can write nice things when only his friends are listening, but try entering the fray with your antagonists. Truth can only be found when your fallacies are hammered at and found wanting. So I write not

expecting much, but at least trying to get my voice, my opinion and perspective out there. Maybe someone will wake up and see that Tom Petty, and for that matter, the rest of our sick celebrity culture are all "emperors with no clothes on."

2. **REKINDLE** the desire to search in others for that which is true, right, lovely and worthwhile. I am not saying I have arrived, but I am saying I have found that when you don't follow the crowd blindly, you see amazing things. I also have found that "Faith" is the only way to see these amazing things—and boy is the view and the rush of truth refreshing.

3. **REFRAME** the way we see God. I have found him, or should I say, in my search, he has found me. I am convinced, God was the one that slowed time down in order to wake me up at the Tom Petty concert. He helped me to see how the "herd of humanity" is being led to the slaughter...and he is nothing like the weak, silly little god I imagined him to be. I think Os Guinness is right, "In short, sin frames God falsely. Thinking of him as he isn't, sin justifies itself in rejecting him as he is...The simple fact is that time and again unbelievers disbelieve in a god that we don't believe in either, a god who isn't like God at all, and a god that we could never believe in a hundred years."

So now I search, but I know what I am searching for. And I also have come to see that the crowd doesn't. For the most part they are caught up with chasing the shadows of entertainment, celebrity, political correctness, 401k balances, a cottage on the lake, fighting for the rights to sleep with who you want, kill human beings that are still in their mother's wombs, stopping terrorism, and trying to figure out how to lynch both Hillary and Donald on the same gallows. We are caught up and obsessed with secondary things...

Chasing shadows, making mud pies, adoring a man who knows what city he is in—there is sooooo much more to the world than this.

I will concede one thing to Tom Petty, he was right when he said, "Don't come around here no more. I've given up..." I have given up finding answers in the crowd. I have stopped going to the same old haunts of drink, debauchery, and popular sentiment that everyone else has set up camp at. I have found a new road, much narrower and yet much more wild and alive. Harder to follow, but easier to fall in love with. Difficult to fully grasp but when touched, even for a second, it is tastier, sweeter, lovelier than anything I have ever experienced.

And I have found some better song lyrics written by a more insightful songwriter than Tom Petty, and his name is Isaiah...

Come, everyone who thirsts, come to the waters; and he who has no money, come, buy and eat! Come, buy wine and milk without money and without price. Why do you spend your money for that which is not bread, and your labor for that which does not satisfy? Listen diligently to me, and eat what is good, and delight yourselves in rich food. Incline your ear, and come to me; hear that your soul may live; Seek the Lord while he may be found; call upon him while he is near!

CHRISTIANITY

THE KINGDOM OF THE KING

"Those who stand for nothing, fall for anything!"

—Alexander Hamilton

Christianity is under assault, truth is, it has always been under assault precisely because it is the truth. Christianity can be described as a set of beliefs, a worldview, guidelines that are predicated on the reality that Christ is King and his followers are citizens of his kingdom. These guidelines teach us how to live to please the King.

But there is a childish movement afoot that involves people who claim loyalty to the King but they don't want to live by the King's rules. They will say, "I love Christ but I can do without Christianity." How foolish!

It is like a 1930's Russian politician who works in the Kremlin saying, "I am Russian leader but I am not going to listen to Stalin." Good luck with that, especially when Stalin had 1,000 of the people in the Politburo shot in cold blood because he didn't trust them.

Christians of every stripe need to be grateful that our King is kind, because he has every right to deny us of our rights. So when you say you are a follower of Christ but not of Christianity you are walking on shaky ground. Christianity is meant to bend our mind and will in service of the King.

Paul says in Colossians 1:9-10, "We continually ask God to fill you with the knowledge of his will through all the wisdom and understanding that the Spirit gives, so that you may live a life worthy of the Lord and please him in every way." That is Christianity!

A Tale of Two Husbands

Written March 6, 2019

"That man who overtook you was Moses, he spareth none, neither knoweth he how to show mercy to those that transgress his Law."
—**Christian from *Pilgrim's Progress***

Every preacher has their favorite illustrations to help explain deep truths. A good story or metaphor can do more for understanding than a complex argument that uses inductive logic, or intricately defines multi-syllable words and theological systematic theories could ever dream of doing.

For me personally, there is one illustration that I love to use that helps explain one of the most troubling issues in the Christian walk: How do you actually live free under grace? As one writer states the problem, "Robust salvation will only occur when you come to the point of understanding where you see that sanctification makes no contribution whatsoever to justification." I agree totally with this proposition, but for most readers, there is no life in this statement, it lands on the heart as cold as a dead fish does on a concrete sidewalk.

So here is a true story that has always stirred my heart while at the same time clarifying what grace filled salvation means.

A lonely woman out of desperation got married. She knew she was getting older, she wanted to have a family, and so she settled. She married a man from her town that had a good job, owned his own house, and he wasn't half-bad looking. The only problem is that he was an angry man. Simmering fury lay just underneath the surface and if he did not get what he wanted when he wanted it he would blow his stack, often throwing things and threatening physical violence toward his wife. He was a miserable man.

Because she was compliant by nature she spent much of her time trying to keep him happy. When he would leave for work he left her a list of things he wanted to be done in the house that day. And by golly, she better do them or the grizzly bear would growl and rage. His list usually consisted of the same "Chores" (with a capital 'C'); cleaning the floors, vacuuming the rugs, polishing the furniture, ironing the clothes, making a tasty dinner, and having paper and slippers waiting.

Every day it was the same thing. Every night trying to keep him satisfied, especially in bed, was getting harder and harder. Thorns of bitterness with deep roots were growing in her heart, her man was mean and she started to hate him. One dark night, his anger finally caught up to him. He had a massive heart attack and died. While the woman was publically mourning she was privately rejoicing.

The bear was dead and she was free.

To occupy her time she got a job at a local business. She was not looking for love because she realized there are worse things than loneliness, like living with an angry man. So she learned to be content in her singleness.

One day, her boss, who was just a few years older than she, stopped at her desk and wondered what she was doing for lunch. They went to a local restaurant and she rather enjoyed his conversation. Thinking nothing of it – it was only lunch after all – she didn't expect it to go further than a friendship. A week later the boss asked her out to dinner, "on a date." A date?

She agreed but was a bit nervous. Never again did she want to get embroiled in a miserable relationship, and even considering re-marriage was out of the question. She told herself to protect her heart. When her boss came to pick her up she was wearing a simple dress and bought an inexpensive pair of new shoes to match. He pulled up, the car was washed, and he looked...dare she say it...quite attractive. "Watch it, don't fall for him!"

They had a great time; the restaurant was on the top floor of a high-priced luxury hotel, the atmosphere was romantic, jazz was playing in the background, and he reserved a private window seat where they could look over the lights on the city. It was a great night. When he dropped her off he turned and said, "By the way, you looked beautiful tonight."

She blushed, and turning toward her house she couldn't believe the words he said, "She looked beautiful." She was not sure she ever heard those words the whole time she was married. After she closed the door, she peeked out the window watching him drive away. "Watch it, don't fall for him!'

The next week she had lunch with him twice, they went on another weekend date, and each outing he complimented her in ways she never heard before. She didn't believe it, she didn't want to believe it. A week turned into a month, a month to six. He kept asking, she kept accepting. And then he got on his knee as they were strolling through a local park...

"Will you marry me?"

She looked deep into his eyes, they were not the angry eyes of her previous husband. This man had kind eyes. Her heart was soaring, so she said, "Yes." The ring slipped easily on her finger, and two months later, the gold band slipped on easily too. The honeymoon was great, and she moved into a new house with her new husband.

For the first few weeks her husband was the picture of

kindness. They would even go back to the restaurant sitting in the same spot looking over the city. He said she looked beautiful again. His kindness didn't stop. And he never got angry.

One day while her new husband was at work, she decided to clean the house. As she was polishing an old desk they brought from her old house, she opened the drawer and out floated an old piece of paper. It was a list of chores from her old husband. Instantly she froze, in her mind, she could see the cold angry eyes of her first husband, they were accusing, judging, condemning. She even heard his voice, "You rotten lazy woman, get to work!'

As she sat on the floor, she looked closely at the list. Never once did her new husband demand that she do any of those things, never once! But she did them for him anyway, in fact, she loved to do them, and she did even more things for him than that were on the list. They were no longer chores, they were acts of love. That night when her husband came home she asked him, "Honey, do I do enough around here? Am I carrying my weight in this marriage?"

"What do you mean?"

"Am I good enough for you?" She dropped her head and sobbing into her hands she dreaded his response. Gently lifting her chin and wiping a tear off her cheek he said, "Now listen to me, I am not your first husband. I have chosen you because I love you. I want you. You are my wife and that is enough." Hugging her tight he whispered in her ear, "You owe me nothing. All I have is yours, and my love for you will never change."

The first husband's name is "Law" "Religion" or "Adam", the second is "Grace", "Relationship" or "Jesus". Listen to what Sinclair Ferguson writes, "Many of us have been permanently marred by that first husband, the despondency that we can never be attractive to our new husband Jesus

Christ, our sliding back into nightmares about our previous 'abusive relationship' – conspires to bring a sense of condemnation. That, in turn, becomes a creeping paralysis in our relationship to the Lord and brings with it a loss of our sense of pardon. We are guilty, failures, ashamed. We must do better to get back into his graces. But we keep failing. We cry to the law to show some mercy; but bare law contains no mercy. It is powerless to pardon...our only hope is to have a clear sight of the nail scars in the hands of Jesus Christ, our second husband."

Now listen to this...

"The abused bride must drink in her new husband's love and fix her eyes on him."

I have a feeling many of you reading feel like the woman who asks, "Am I good enough for you?" Jesus gently shows you his nail pierced hand and asks you, "Am I enough for you?"

He is for me!

Our Love Affair with Woodstock

Written January 17, 2019

This year marks the 50th Anniversary of Woodstock. What was originally billed as three days of "Peace, Love, and Music" has become the primary symbol of a watershed moment in modern American cultural life. When people think of the sixties they think of Woodstock. Little did the organizers of this haphazardly planned outdoor music festival know just how influential it was to become. The music and images recorded from those three days have been seared on all of our collective psyches.

Woodstock has come to mean many different things to many different people. For some, celebrating peace and love was like opening a window in a musty old house, "Ah finally, fresh air!". For others, Woodstock and the pulsating mass of jeans and halter-top wearing teenagers offered fodder for the starched collared morality police who believed that America was now rotten to the core. Some saw Woodstock as the highpoint of rock music where artistic freedom was allowed to flourish; untainted by the commercialization that is now ruining the music industry. Others can barely get past the suffocating green haze created by platoons of pot smoking flower children.

Woodstock occurred when I was a two-year-old boy. But for my oldest sister, she remembered it all – – and hearing about the hundreds of thousands of young people camping out at a farmer's field listening to the most popular musicians and poets of the time made quite an impression on her. She soon adopted the hippie fashions of bell bottom pants and tie-dye t-shirts. I also remember her "keep on trucking" patch, and now whenever I see pictures of yellow and blue Volkswagen vans painted with peace signs on the side it reminds me of her. The Woodstock culture makes me smile. So on a personal level, I find the whole topic of Woodstock incredibly fascinating.

But it is the sociological questions that interest me the most, why was Woodstock so captivating? There have been scores of outdoor music festivals, hippie love-ins, and pot smoking parties, but Woodstock stands out above them all. Why? Why is everyone still wanting to re-enact the nostalgia of Woodstock in festivals like Burning Man and Coachella? And it has to be more than the pictures of naked people rolling in mud and Jimi Hendrix playing the electric guitar while his mile-high afro is shining brightly in the hot August sun.

I think the answer lies in the fact that more than anything else, Woodstock exposed very clearly to the watching world the generational clash of ideas. Like the massive waves off of Cape Horn, where the winds of the Andes mountains beat down upon the colliding edges of the Atlantic and Pacific Oceans; Woodstock was a war of two worldviews. The new ideas of the young clashed and hurled themselves against the seemingly rock hard immovable ideals of the old guard. While one worldview was dying, Modern pragmatism (legalism), a new thought pattern was emerging, Post-modern utopianism (antinomianism).

Os Guinness describes the mindset of Woodstock and the sixties like this in his book, *The Dust of Death*, "The United States reached the climax of a generation-long crisis of cultural authority – the beliefs, ideals, and traditions that once shaped Americans lost their compelling power." Woodstock was the defining cultural moment when the post-WW2 children were growing up and no longer wanted the world their parents created. They wanted to break the constricting chains of authoritarian conformity and celebrate the freedom to create new norms and modes of self-expression as they saw fit.

The only problem, as we will see, is that both views have their origins in arbitrary man-made values and aspirations which has no way to offer real long term meaning and hope.

When it comes to the dying generational mindset that led to Woodstock, one writer named Jules Henry in his 1962 book Culture against Man, called it "the Indo-European, Islamic, Hebraic Impulse-control system." This impulse-control system was all about placing limits and constraints on people in order to achieve order and desired outcome. It was behaviorism plain and simple. Shared uniformity of values was the goal. Robert Bly in the book, *The Sibling Society* says this about it, "The impulse-control system smelled of limitation; schools stank of it. It reeked of the bald, the severe, the cabined, the icebound, the squat, the cramped, the dinky, the narrow, the scanty, the roped-in, the meager, the bad, the tame. Above everything sat the parental or institutional tyrant, the one with the thin nose, a black coat, and steel-rimmed glasses, the one who had told them in grade school to sit down, to behave, to hold their bodies stiffly, to salute the flag and stand up when a teacher enters the room."

One English observer who visited the United States in the late 50's said, "there was an extraordinary desire of American grown-ups to be respected and loved by thier children. But they didn't seem to feel it necessary to love in return; rather, to be the object of love was all that was required."

This old way of life tried to hide the general dissatisfaction with the sterile order under plastered smiles and little pink houses snuggled together in pristine subdivisions. A perfect storm was brewing, Beaver Cleaver could no longer contain his rage. Rules without a loving relationship stir up deep anger and bitterness in the heart, and when the new winds of the '60s came, Woodstock offered a visual picture of "what could be" , and it unleashed a whirlwind.

So what has replaced the "impulse-control system?" And is the new system any better? The young generation was hoping that "Peace, Love and Music" would foster in the brotherhood of man, and what they got in return was rule by pop-culture. Parents and teachers no longer set the rules, Hendrix, Baez and Jagger did. There will always be a need for a hero to fill the vacuum that the tyrant left, and the hero is now the celebrity.

Robert Bly writes, "Unjust severity had been overcome or bypassed. Fundamentalist harshness, Marxist rigidity, the stiff ethic of high school superintendents, had passed away. People greeted each other, clothed or naked, in delight, feeling that a victory of humanness was won. With the help of rock music, young men and women felt freed from a parental or institutional tyrant..."

Woodstock demanded unrestrained freedom. The pendulum had swung, but in its path, the new generation had no mercy for the important values that were beneficial in the old system. If the Rolling Stones thumbed their nose at the importance of 'delayed gratification' and 'parental respect' because they "couldn't get no satisfaction", it was also a call for all young people to *"stick it to the man"*, as Jack Black would say. So what did the new generation want?

Doing what was right, or doing what feels right?

What feels right won the day, and is still on the throne, "...lighthearted, open to impulses rising from below his belt, playful, and yet grounded in sexuality, heavier than Peter Pan...it felt as if human beings were able for the first time in history to choose their own roads, choose what to do with their own bodies, choose the visionary possibilities formerly shut off by the 'control system.'"

That sounds all well and good, but what possibilities did they choose? What did the pop-culture offer them? We've spent the last 50 years trying to figure that out, and the results are not simply "Peace, Love, and Music"; a new task master has arrived, popularity! As one writer has said, "It is hard to be as popular as we are supposed to be." And who decided if I am as popular as I should be? I do, of course.

And I am never satisfied.

The psychologist Giles Lipovetsy says, "We demand of ourselves fame and success which, it not achieved, unleashes an implacable storm of criticism against the self." This is why we chant the useless mantra, "In order to forgive others, we must first forgive ourselves." But forgiveness is hard to achieve when I don't get as many likes on my selfie, or I see on Facebook how my strawberry salad does not look as nice as my besties does that she just posted. Robert Bly makes the case that our inward drive for fame and success is a worse tyrant than the high school superintendent ever was, "If a teenager is not invited to the dance, she may try suicide. A high school boy, scoffed at, may retreat behind his computer for ten years."

He finishes with this sad statement, "In the past, the authoritarian Judge demanded obedience to parents, and insisted on sexual "purity," and, one could say, advocated for high morals. But now, the one who fails to become successful and well loved, punishment is swift and thorough. Self receives a battering from the inside, everyone feels insignificant and unseen, until, in desperation, we finally agree to go on a talk show and tell it all."

So what is the answer? In the book, *The Whole Christ*, Sinclair Ferguson argues that both "legalism" (rule under arbitrary manmade laws) and "antinomianism" (rule by self) come from the same place when he says, "Legalism and antinomianism are, in fact, non-identical twins that emerge from the same womb…Both of them are a restricted heart disposition of God." I would take it a step further and say that both fail because they leave out the one who gives life any significance, Jesus Christ.

Scripture says in 2 Corinthians 4:4, "The god of this age has blinded the minds of unbelievers, so that they cannot see the light of the gospel that displays the glory of Christ, who is the image of God." In other words, Satan, a real being who hates God, wants all people to see God as forbidding and restrictive, kind of like an "institutional tyrant, the one with the thin nose, a black coat, and steel-rimmed glasses." And like the Woodstock generation, he wants us to declare complete freedom and independence from him hoping to rule ourselves.

But true "Peace, Love and Music" can only found in the one who is love. Don't let daisy chains of flowers and a peace sign fool you, without God, unrestrained freedom leads to a worse tyranny than the man wearing the steel-rimmed glasses could ever bring about.

Arguing With Augustine

Written January 21, 2014

A couple of days after I started writing this blog, Derek Max came into my office, looking cool & confused, and posited the question, "Chris, what's your point, why are you writing a blog, and who are you trying to argue with?"

Argue? I am not trying to argue...or am I? Maybe I am, but with whom? And what does it really accomplish because everyone is right these days...and we are all entitled our opinions because all of our opinions are valid...aren't they? And why does Derek have to spoil my fun? RAT-FINK!

As I have been mulling these questions over in my mind I was studying Saint Augustine's treatise on "De Trinitate" (The Trinity) written in 371 a.d. Ironically, he addressed the exact same issue of argument and its purpose, because "De Trinitate" was an argument to prove Christ's deity. In the year 325 the Council of Nicaea established Christ's absolute equality with the Father as orthodoxy for true Christian teaching. But that didn't stop the battle for doctrine to stop raging because there were still large pockets of Arians and Sabellians who were teaching their followers to deny the full divinity of the Son. And to say both sides were right was just wrong! So Augustine took up his pen to both show how New Testament scripture supported Nicaea's teaching and to silence the loud voices of opposition. We probably can't even imagine the fury and violence felt between both factions. So Augustine, in his introduction, addresses the people who would rather fume and bluster than reasonably think.

"We must first establish *by the authority of the holy*

scriptures that our teaching is true. Only then shall we go on, if God so wills and gives his help, to accommodate those who have more conceit than capacity, which makes the disease they suffer from all the more dangerous...perhaps [through scripture] they are able to discover reasons they can have no doubt about...they will sooner find fault with their own minds than with the truth itself or our arguments."

More conceit than capacity: in other words, many of the people we try to have discussions/arguments with will often be confident of their position not based on reason, but on who they think they are. That is why he says God has to help them with the "disease they suffer from." What is that disease? Pride. Sometimes because people have a degree, the color of their skin is different, they drank a beer, or they have moved out of mom and dad's house, they think they know everything. And the rest of the world, well, they are morons! Proud people are blinded by their own pride, and when you try to have a civil argument with a proud person you lose the argument even before you open your mouth.

Augustine decides to keep arguing anyway, even if he is surrounded by conceited critics, because he thinks it can still help save and rescue people, "If there is a particle of the love or fear of God in them, they may return to the beginning and right order of faith." Hopefully, through honest well-articulated debate, we can steer people back onto the path. Open dialogue also demands that we also must be willing to be corrected by the critic. Argument and contention have always been around; and even though it may get heated, I think we still owe it to people to tell the truth and point out error. I thank God for writers who have corrected me, taught me, rebuked me. The shallow soul is the person who sees someone heading over a cliff and fails to warn because they don't want to cause conflict.

I love how Augustine ends his discussion on the

argument, "I should prefer to be censured by the censurer of falsehood than to receive its praiser's praises." In other words, it is a good thing to make proud foolish people mad at you; because if you stay safe so they agree with you, you become part of the party of fools! Courage requires you to stick your neck out knowing someone is going to try to chop it off.

WINE: Is the Devil Inside?

Written March 7, 2014

Oh no, what every pastor dreads, it's time to preach on John 2: "But how could Jesus do this to me; did he even think through the difficulties that would arise when he turned water into wine? So many troubling questions? Maybe we can just leave out this chapter entirely, no one will notice?" Sadly, the nature of the church beast is to read John 2 and then quickly jump to argument and dispute concerning the questionable alcoholic content of the wine. (Was it grape juice? Low alcoholic content: 10 parts water and 1 part wine, or maybe Jesus changed it for medicinal reasons so the guests at the party wouldn't get sick?) Only in America does this issue stir such passionate debate. I spent a year in Russia and they served champagne for lunch in the kindergarten teachers lounge while we were showing the "Jesus Film" and no one gave it a second thought...no big deal.

This debate reminds me of a wedding I attended 10 years ago: while getting some punch for my wife and me, a church member was standing next to me watching as the bartender was serving beer from the tap. He turned to me and quietly muttered under his breath, "Look, the devil is staring at us out of that cup." I looked at him and said, "I didn't know plastic could hold him so easily; don't worry, I think the devil has better places to be tonight."

So is the devil in the drink?

And if he is, what does Jesus have to say for himself when he made over 150 gallons of the "best vintage" wine to keep the festivities going at a wedding party? How could Jesus, the holy one, make something that could cause someone to sin? (And while we are asking, was Jesus promoting gluttony when he fed the 5,000? Was he promoting adultery when he let a prostitute wash his feet with her hair?) Surely there must be an answer that makes everyone happy? Well...there isn't. Here is why...

1. Jesus made actual alcoholic wine, there is no way getting around it. (Ephesians 5:18 uses the same Greek word for wine as John 2—and this verse offers indirect proof that this wine is fermented because you can get drunk on it.)

2. True lovers of God are not to get drunk on it, for it is sin & you won't inherit heaven. (1 Cor. 6:10) So a word to the grace abuser: Stop being a drinking hero and bragging about your ability to hold your liquor (Isaiah 5:22), and please don't let alcohol find you for a fool (Proverbs 23:29 -35). What God asks of us is to allow him to reveal Christ in our lives (Gal. 1:15-16), and we do this by becoming a godly noble adult who exercises self-control (Gal. 5:23). So grow up and quit glorying in your shame (Phil. 3:19).

3. The final truth that is often missed and forgotten is that wine actually is a gift, it is given to lift the heart of man (Psalm 104:15). In our zeal to prove our purity and our capacity for self-denial through praise-worthy human effort, we disallow and condemn some things that God wanted us to have for good. The question in everything we do is the matter of, "Am I exercising 'proper use' or 'abuse?'" Did you know it is possible to drink too much coffee and Mountain Dew? (I know the pounding headaches of "abuse" first hand).

So this debate will continue to rage, people will continue

to argue it till God's kingdom comes. But what is lost in the smoke of the on-going cannon fire is that discerning the exact level of alcoholic content in the "best vintage" wine has absolutely nothing to do with the message of John 2. In our myopic fuss, we miss the point of the story completely! Jesus turning water (ceremonial jars for purification) into wine is a statement of how he now offers his new life to us by grace. He has come to totally fulfill the law, just like he had the water pots filled to the brim; and now he asks you to draw out of his completed work on our behalf, this new, substantial, "best vintage" life by faith (Isaiah 12:3).

I once heard a person say, "I wish Jesus never turned water into wine because it makes things so complicated." Consider that statement a second, someone has the gall to question the decisions made by the Lord of Glory! Who do we think we are?

If Jesus wants to turn water into wine, I think he knows what he is doing. Why can't we simply learn to fall on our knees in worship and wonder, "What a wonderful, creative, dangerous God!"

IT BURNS! & assorted other lies…

Written March 10, 2014

Amazing! My last post generated 10x the hits than any other post I published so far. I wonder why? I can speculate: "Hmm, maybe there are a lot of secret scalawags out there who are looking for biblical justification to keep sipping on their Rum? I know…I am being stalked by heretic hunters who want to take down another renegade liberal 'wolf-in-sheep's-clothing' pastor? Or maybe people simply want to know what the Bible actually says about difficult subjects instead of just walking lock-step in man-made tradition?" Whatever the reason, the amount of perusers to my last post excites me. Not because I want to be popular; but as a pastor, I want people to think! Proper biblical interpretation and application are vital if Christians are to gain wisdom and understanding. God's goal is for us to live as mature adults who are characterized by a "sound mind with self-discipline." (2 Tim. 1:7) For far too long, churches had developed adolescent followers who make "fear-based" reactionary decisions…let me give you a hyperbolic example of what I mean (exaggeration for the purpose of illustration):

Let's say you are a mom who is just trying to maintain sanity in a claustrophobic house with two highly active toddlers who are "driving you crazy." While you are preparing "SpongeBob" Mac-n-Cheese on the stove for lunch, your phone rings in your bedroom upstairs. As the water begins to boil, and seeing that your kids are throwing Lego's at each other in the living room, you have a very serious decision to make: "Do I run quickly upstairs to get my phone, or let it go so my kids don't come in here and burn their fingers on the hot stove, or even worse, dump a pot of boiling water on their head?" Since you are a well-meaning mom, you make a split-second decision: "I know, I will tell my kids not to go into the kitchen at all because the floor is so hot 'It Burns!' Yeah, that will keep them far away from the stove." So after you tell them how they will be fried to a crisp by just touching the kitchen floor, you run upstairs, grab your phone and happily answer it in time. "Mrs. Smith, congratulations, you won a 3 day all expense paid vacation to Scranton, Pennsylvania to visit Dunder Mifflin." Yes, you finally won, and your little story worked! As you go back downstairs your kids are frozen in complete fear as they stare into the dark horror room called "the kitchen." "Ahhhhh, it worked, my story will now keep my children alive for another five years. Now that is called responsible parenting!"

Or is it?

What happens when one kid notices that after they chased the kitten into the kitchen, it didn't fry? "Hmm, Chocolate Puff is still alive? Maybe the kitchen floor isn't that hot after all." So out of curiosity, your child touches a bare toe on the linoleum floor, and, nothing happens. He then bursts into the kitchen and starts running all around realizing that they are survivors! In their little brain they wonder, "Maybe, just maybe, mommy was not telling me the whole truth? Or she doesn't know how invincible I am?" And then your child becomes convinced of their new super-powers of survival; they then see water bubbling on a cool orange glowing circle as a new challenge, and think to themselves, "Mommy told me not to touch that either...but I will survive!" Not good!

Ridiculous story, I know, but it uses the same kind of logic many people in the church have been raised on in order to avoid the dangers of this world:

- Mixed bathing is a no, no. It leads to touching and touching leads to …

- No movie theatres because you are promoting the Hollywood lifestyle and everything that goes with it. Do you want to fund Sodom and Gomorrah? "Well, didn't you just have me over to watch the "Avengers" on DVD?" Yeah, but that is different…

- Dancing leads to swaying which leads to hugging which leads to grinding which leads to ….

- You may have the sort of tongue that once it touches a drop of alcohol, your eyes glaze over and you turn instantly into a person with an unstoppable addiction, and soon you will become a night-stalking zombie craving drink upon drink…

- Rock n Roll has drumbeats that come from the jungles of Africa, which leads to pagan demon worship, and leads to….

- Hanging around Calvinists will cause you to stop loving people and see life in categories and boxes, and you will only grow tulips in your garden….

Do you see how we have been taught to make decisions out of fear? Fear makes us stupid, there is no way around it. God has given us the mind of Christ, he has given us the power of the Spirit…what shall we fear? Some of you are saying: "Yeah but you are a leader and we must set up boundaries to stop impure behavior." But here is my problem with that statement: what happens when our boundaries are not biblical and a person steps over them and realizes we were not accurate? Well, sadly, sometimes when we finally do teach biblical truth, it is ignored and treated as another false boundary.

That is why I believe hell is no longer feared! Because rock music, movie theaters and alcohol weren't as hot as we previously warned; and maybe, just maybe, hell won't be so bad after all?

Truth & Cement: (Pt 1: Pluralism's Poison)

Written March 19, 2014

Wednesdays on this blog involve discussing whatever is on my mind...a space to talk about something that I am deeply interested in. And for the next 4 or 5 Wednesdays, I am going to hammer on a theme entitled "Truth & Cement." (I invite you to join me if you don't mind listening to someone discuss & debate with himself.) Personally speaking, I have been on a hunt for something my whole life, "honest truth." I am growing weary with trying to keep up with the newest theological imaginings, cool church trends, and post-modern constructs that don't seem to clarify understanding; but rather confuse and weaken what once seemed firm. Convictions are so easily sacrificed these days on the altar of tolerance and "niceness." We want intellectuals, actors and angry women to like us so we temper our opinions and seek to prove how "open minded" we are. If someone believes the sky has a Scottish plaid-green pattern, we no longer can disagree with a look of incredulity; but now we are only allowed to look up at the clouds and smile admiring their fascinating insight. The ultimate goal of an advanced society is to find common ground in order to dialogue and seek to understand the world's wonderful diversity of ideas.

D. A. Carson in his book "The Gagging of God," talks about the poisonous influence that philosophical pluralism is having on the search for truth, "Any notion that a particular ideological or religious claim is intrinsically superior to another is necessarily wrong...If all interpretation is culturally conditioned it becomes a tool for domination." Therefore, he explains, in the mind of the post-modern scholar, "no interpretation can be dismissed, and no interpretation can be allowed the status of objective truth!" In the classroom of the University this sort of conclusion displays the brilliance of an open and fertile mind, but in the real world, this is a load of cow manure.

Let me show you what I mean from something I learned first-hand working with simple bricklayers. How you mix cement, specifically when it comes to adding the proper amount of sand, really, really matters. To the novice laborer, mixing cement seems rather trivial—but not to the journeyman mason. You must mix it right! Too much sand makes it weak, not enough makes it stiff and unusable. I was talking with one seasoned construction veteran and he told me his dad taught him how to mix it just right. This basic formula was passed down from his dad, who learned it from his dad, who learned it from his dad. So I asked him, "Don't you think it is time to come up with a new way of mixing cement? Try shifting the focus, look for a new "cement paradigm": switch up the ingredients, try changing the mixing ratios of sand, cement, lime and water? You never know how much better and efficient you will be until you try?"

He said, "Do you want a wall that stays standing for years or one that falls apart at the first hint of rain?" I said one that stands. He said, "Then do it my way: it has been rigorously tested, it has stood strong through years of wear and tear. This cement formula has more than proven itself!"

Is he intolerant? YES! Is his opinion superior? YES! Is his opinion unreasonable? No! He lives in the real world, and he knows what "truly" works. This is what I am on the search for in all things religious. I am tired of cool square rimmed glasses guys coming around saying, "Try putting some more sand in your atonement theory. Maybe your exclusive eschatology is formed from your modernist perspective?

Salvation is much more fluid than believing you simply need to be "Born Again." We need to catch up with the times, isn't it about time to let the old doctrines go? That ship has sailed." Or, "Hey, isn't it about time to stop calling heresy, heresy and start letting all new ideas, new paradigms, and fresh re-imagined constructs to have an equal voice at the table of dialogue?"

It all depends: Do you want your faith to "stand for years" or fall apart at the first sign of rain? So if you are willing, come with me on Wednesdays as we go back to learn some basic skills of cement mixing. I want my faith to stand...

HOW ABOUT YOU?

Cement & Truth: (Pt 2: God Speaks)

Written March 26, 2014

Here we go with the topics that I consider to be the "cement" or binding "mortar" for establishing a strong, life-giving faith. I believe these things to be "true truth" and the essential foundation stones if you want to grow in maturity. The first foundation stone for me is this: "God has spoken to us and he still speaks…and he made us perfectly able to understand his speech." In other words, I believe God really wants to communicate with us, and he isn't playing games with language; he speaks clearly and directly. I have a funny illustration that perfectly frames this discussion:

Last Wednesday, my original post generated many interesting comments on Facebook. In the back and forth dialogue there was a lot of "Highfalutin" (Def: seeming or trying to seem great or important) words used to sound intelligent. Words like "new hermeneutic", "modern constructs", "existentialism", and "sophistry". (Sadly, most of these words were used by me so I gave off the impression to those who also like to give off scholarly impressions, that I read and understand "highfalutin" words.) Well, later that day a person who was following the discussion came up to me and said, "I didn't understand half of what was being said. Can you dumb it down for some of us next time?" This humble request was both an appropriate and brilliant example of the desire of people to "truly connect when communicating." In fact, all of us expect other people to speak to us in a way that makes sense. If you didn't, you would never read blogs in the first place.

So if human beings can adjust their language so ideas are transmitted with accuracy and clarity, don't you think God can exercise the same ability? Some post-modern scholars aren't too sure about this; they think God is so unlike us that he is unable to be properly understood. But my contention today is that since God made us, he knows exactly how to communicate with us! So when we are looking for meaning, purpose and clear explanations I believe God has spoken and still speaks—he is not playing a game of "Hide-n-Go-Seek" with us, he loves it when we seek for truth (Isaiah 55:6)

Psalm 19:1-9 discusses how God speaks through two clear vehicles: 1. Nature (verse 3) – "There is no speech or language where their voice is not heard. Their voice goes out into all the earth." The beauty of the earth, the wonder of the heavens, the brilliant fine-tuning of the ecosystem displays the mind of a genius. Sure, people try to explain it away by random chance, but deep down in the gut of a human's soul… people know God did this. So why is there such a huge movement to push God out of public discourse, to mock "Intelligent Design," to force a monolithic mind-meld concerning evolution? Simple: "Out of sight, out of mind." God's invisibility allows for the prideful man to believe his own lies about his delusion of "supposed" greatness. (Read Romans 1:18-25 if you don't believe me).

That is why God communicated through 2. His Word (verse 7) – "The law of the Lord is perfect, reviving the soul." God's word is perfect in that it accurately represents reality, as it is. And it is perfect in the sense that it speaks to us on our level—it is designed to be understood. Yes, God is Infinite, Holy, and Transcendent (above us in every way); but he knows how we think because he made our brain. When a dad talks to his 2-year-old daughter does he use words like "existentialism", "sophistry", and "hermeneutics"? Of course not, he speaks in a language that perfectly connects with the mind of his daughter, and they have a real relationship. (Sometimes it is easier to communicate with a 2-year-old as compared to an 18-year-old). So why don't people understand God's word? Why does it seem so confusing? Here is my simple, non-highfalutin reply: "People don't want to communicate, they have better things to do."

Very simply:

1. God's Word can be understood (Luke 1:1-4); however, you must put forth some effort to understand it (2 Timothy 2:15). I don't buy it when people say the words are too big, the concepts too fuzzy, it's too confusing. Just ask them questions in their area of interest: Computer geeks use big words: "Gigabyte", "Active-Matrix", "Hexidecimal". Social savvy teens have their own language: BTW, CU L8R, FOCL. Brainless football fans: "Line of Scrimmage", "Intentional Grounding", "2 Gap 3-4 Defensive Schemes." To find gold you must dig.

2. God's Word is never presented as a fairy tale, it is meant to be read seriously. Peter says he didn't invent this (2 Peter 1:16); John says he saw Jesus with his very own eyes (1 John 1:1-3); the Old Testament writers often didn't want to speak but they had to (Jer. 20:7-9). Proper communication must respect the intent of the person speaking. If I told you something serious, "My dad died," and you said that "I was speaking in a vague poetic genre that was open to a wide variety of interpretations dependent on the 'cultural community' of the time of my utterance", I would punch you right in the nose. The reason I would punch you is that you were purposely not trying to understand me!

3. Finally, and this must be heard, God's word is dangerous; don't play around with it. 2 Peter 3:16 says if you purposely distort it's meaning you will be destroyed. Proverbs 30:6 says God will defend its trustworthiness, and Revelation 22:18-19 says that ... well...read it for yourself, it scares me too much to talk about.

It isn't complicated: decay in society, destruction of families, explosion of perversity, moral and intellectual ruin, even poverty all begins with the "lack of delight in God's Word". (Jeremiah 6:10).

I want to close on a perfect example of how, when left alone to our own devices, humans use language to complicate things, not make them clear. Just recently Gwyneth Paltrow & Chris Martin separated after 10 years of marriage. Scripture is very clear on its warning: "God hates divorce." But no, not in our sophisticated day and age; divorce is a much more complex issue. Listen to this article from Dr. Habib Sadeghi and Dr. Sherry Sami: "when the whole concept of marriage and divorce is reexamined, there's actually something far more powerful—and positive—at play." The doctors consider how insects might be able to tell us something about divorce. They write:

"The misunderstandings involved in divorce also have much to do with the lack of intercourse between our own internal masculine and feminine energies. Choosing to hide within an endoskeleton and remain in attack mode requires a great imbalance of masculine energy. Feminine energy is the source of peacemaking, nurturing, and healing. Cultivating your feminine energy during this time is beneficial to the success of conscious uncoupling. When our masculine and feminine energies reach equilibrium once more, we can emerge from our old relationship and consciously call in someone who reflects our new world, not the old one." That is why they called their divorce: "Conscious Uncoupling."

So you tell me, who is easier to understand, God or our "enlightened" experts?

Cement & Truth: (Pt 3: Doubt, Being Human & Biting Snakes)

Written March 28, 2014

What do you do? Your 13-year-old daughter sits down at the kitchen table and asks you this question, "Dad, I am not sure if God really exists. How do you believe in someone you can't see?" As a Christian parent, especially a pastor, should you tell her in harsh tones to "just believe"? Do you put your hands on your face and ask her mournfully where you have failed as a parent? Or do you thank God that your daughter feels the freedom to share her doubts with you about God?

"Sharing doubts? Isn't that dangerous, isn't that encouraging sin?"

No, doubting is not sin, it is a part of being human. Think about it, if doubt wasn't normal why would we be told to live by faith? Part of being human is our limited capacity in knowing all things fully, we don't see hardly anything clearly. In our study of John, even after talking with Jesus face to face about spiritual things, Nicodemus, the brilliant teacher, was still full of doubt and confusion. The truth is, from living in this broken world we are placed in a land that is awash in doubt. Our problem is not doubt, it is our response to it. There are two "foolish" ways to deal with it when it arises:

1. Out of fear, you completely ignore doubt and act as if it doesn't exist.

2. Out of pride, you relish it and act superior because it proves you are an "independent thinker."

Both approaches are deadly because, like a poisonous snake, doubt will bite you! And when it does it leads a soul toward "confirmed unbelief." So what every person must do is go to war to de-fang the snake of doubt. (You can really never kill it, but you can render it harmless). How? Let me diagram it (this concept I gleaned from Oz Guinness in his book "God in the Dark"):

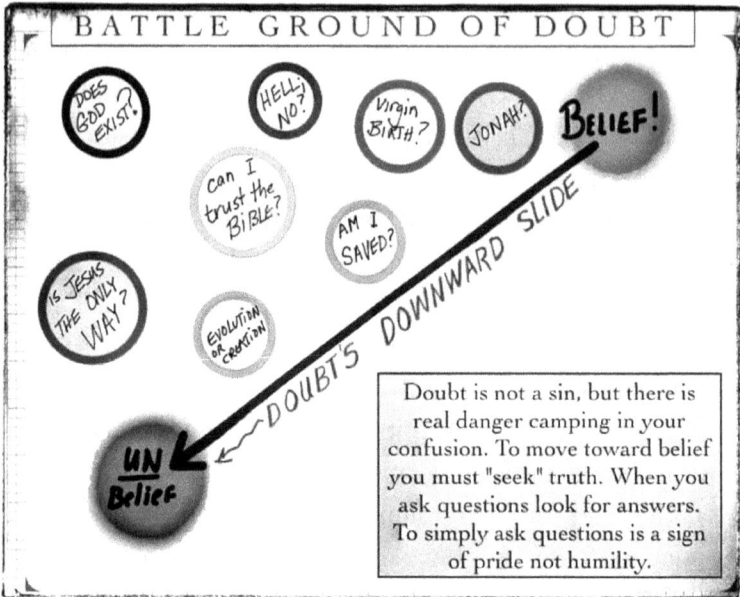

BATTLE GROUND OF DOUBT

DOES GOD EXIST?

HELL? NO?

Virgin BIRTH?

JONAH?

BELIEF!

Can I trust the BIBLE?

AM I SAVED?

DOUBT'S DOWNWARD SLIDE

IS JESUS THE ONLY WAY?

EVOLUTION or CREATION

UN Belief

Doubt is not a sin, but there is real danger camping in your confusion. To move toward belief you must "seek" truth. When you ask questions look for answers. To simply ask questions is a sign of pride not humility.

1. Doubt Exists: You can not wish it, hope it, or dream doubt away—the human heart is seeking certainty all of its life, it never stops. Why else does your wife want to know, almost daily, if you love her? Because doubt exists. And this is never more true than in the abstract realm of faith. Like Doubting Thomas, "We want to feel Christ's wounds with our own hands." I thank God Thomas has the "HOOTSVAH" to ask Jesus if he can touch! On the diagram I have listed many different areas we doubt—they are real, and it is not a sin to wonder about these

things.

2. Doubts, when left unchallenged, slide toward unbelief. Unbelief is the sin: God has answers, he rewards seekers, he has sent his Son. But if we ignore all he has done, and choose to remain independent, we follow in the cursed path that Adam wrought on this earth. One of the biggest "smokescreens" in this battle is when people ask questions, not to find answers, but to sound intelligent. True seekers will be given answers, but when the answers are given they must treat them as gold; answers are direct invitations by God to "Come and See."

3. When you do "Come and See," faith is strengthened; and you will soon find that the road to belief is paved with solid stone. If you struggle with belief, read the following quote by F. Gerrit Immink that discusses how God builds faith through doubt:

"Faith stands in a constant tension between human trust and divine trustworthiness. God's truth is that God is true, that is, trustworthy and utterly dependable. And this is where our faith finds its certainty: in who God is. It is not a blind trust but a trust that is linked to what we know and understand. This naturally means a believer must nurture his relationship to grow in knowledge. As a result, believers face a continuous struggle against their own unbelief. After a while, the certainty they do achieve does not result from a rational proof but from a persuasion of divine truth."

Let me ask you this question: When there is a court trial to convict someone of a crime, what is the goal of the prosecution in order to gain a conviction? "To prove that the crime occurred BEYOND A REASONABLE DOUBT." It is not to prove a crime occurred with "100% CERTAINTY."

Doubt will always exist, but that doesn't mean we can't find a firm base to trust. In fact, as you read this you sat down on your chair because there was a strong chance it would hold you up even though you weren't perfectly certain it would.

So, what happened with the 13-year-old daughter? I spent a good hour and a half walking through the book of 1 Corinthians 15 with her, and it was one of the greatest conversations we ever had. Having your daughter read the writings of Paul and how 500 people witnessed the risen Christ is a privilege for any father.

Don't doubt me on that!

What If Christianity Doesn't Work?

Written March 16, 2016

Two days ago, one of my biggest fears became reality. My daughter looked at me right in the eyes wearing a very serious, almost desperate expression on her face; and in fear and trepidation she asked me, "Dad, have you ever heard of Joel Osteen?"

My heart stopped. I thought to myself, "Noooooooooo, not him?" I have done everything I could to shelter my sweet innocent daughter from the terrors of this harsh world, and now she has run smack into one of the vilest enemies to a God -pleasing life: Sappy, Plastic, Delusionally-Positive, Name it-Claim it Christianity.

After gathering my wits, I replied, "Why do you ask?"

"Because a lady at work found out I was a Christian and she said, 'Oh I love Joel Osteen, I have all his books, and I watch all his sermons. Do you like him?'" My daughter replied to her, "I never heard of him, but I am sure my dad has, he is a pastor."

The lady's eyes drooped and then she said, "Oh...he probably won't like him...Joel doesn't really use the Bible too much, he is not that deep, but his teaching works for me...it makes me feel good. And I love his suits."

Hmmm..."Makes me feel good...His teaching works for me." What does that mean? And is this the goal of Christianity, having it work for you? And what if it doesn't work for me, should I just quit and go do something else, believe something else? Should I even stop trusting in Jesus?

American culture runs on pragmatism. This is the belief

that if something works for me, helps me get what I want, brings me success, it must be right and true. Progress in my personal life is all that matters, and pragmatism is the philosophy that gets me there. Progress for Joel Osteen is being the "Best You" you can be. Including being happy, healthy, successful, having a great smile and being everyone's best friend. And for many Christian pragmatists, this is the reason Jesus came to earth. To get you what you want.

Just open your bible, pray the right positive words, do the right things and everything will go your way. Jesus promises.

But what if it doesn't? There are two heretical (bad and dangerous teaching) schools of thought on how to make sense of the world when things don't go your way:

1. It is a sign you don't have enough faith. Some churches actually teach that most of people's troubles are their own fault. If they only would trust God without doubting, life would "work." Meaning riches would fall from the sky, miraculous healing would occur and that house you always wanted would be yours. And if those things are not taking place you aren't really speaking positivity into the world and then believing. That is what some people even told my parents after they met my sister who has a debilitating disease called "Rhett's Syndrome." They blamed my mom and dad for her sad state; my parents were not exercising enough faith. I have never seen my dad so hot!

2. It is a sign those rotten demons are at it again. We are told they sneak, hide in the shadows and are the primary cause of your miserable life. All you need to do is get some expert to "deliver" you or teach you how to say the right words to bind them in chains of spiritual steel, and voilà they will leave and your life will become

wonderful again. Boy, it sure is a shame how the Holy Spirit in you can't stop those pesky demons. But once they are gone, you can once again look forward to your rainbow in the sky.

But what if the bible has never promised you a rose garden? What if the bible actually says, "In this life you will have trouble" (See John 16:33)? What if some of your prayers never come true and success doesn't fall in your lap—has God failed you? Is he no longer to be believed or worshiped?

Right after my daughter asked me about Joel Osteen I was reading my Psalm for the day, it was Psalm 44. Listen to verses 8-17, I am not sure they are in the pragmatist's bible:

In God we have boasted continually,
and we will give thanks to your name forever. Selah
But you have rejected us and disgraced us
and have not gone out with our armies.
You have made us turn back from the foe,
and those who hate us have gotten spoil.
You have made us like sheep for slaughter
and have scattered us among the nations.
You have sold your people for a trifle,
demanding no high price for them.
You have made us the taunt of our neighbors,
the derision and scorn of those around us.
You have made us a byword among the nations,
a laughingstock among the peoples.
All day long my disgrace is before me,
and shame has covered my face
at the sound of the taunter and reviler,
at the sight of the enemy and the avenger.
All this has come upon us,
though we have not forgotten you,

and we have not been false to your covenant.

I have found that true worship is believing even when things are not working. In the same way, I have also found that even though it may be raining the sun is still shining behind the clouds.

I don't believe in God because it works, I believe in God because he is God. Asking if Christianity works may be the most simplistic, narcissistic and silliest question you could ever ask. But that is America for you, everything is always about us, and truth is only found on the other side of success.

Somehow, we have bought the lie that Jesus may have suffered on the cross, but it is so I could sit on my big, fat comfy couch for all eternity asking him to keep serving me while I watch my favorite Netflix series on my heavenly TV. He gets utter humiliation, I get abundance. It's only fair, right?

And I know that the TV I watch in heaven will never break down because God is a pragmatist. He works.

The Most Ludicrous Lie Some Christians Tell Themselves

Written April 1, 2016

Therefore we know that it is the last hour. They went out from us, but they were not of us; for if they had been of us, they would have continued with us. But they went out, that it might become plain that they all are not of us.

(1 John 2:18-19)

It sounds so daring, so dangerous, so brave...but it is nothing more than a lie told by those who want their freedom to be unhindered and applauded. No commitment or responsibility, all options kept open. What is the lie you ask? Well it can be couched in many different forms, but the main one is this:

"I love Jesus, but I don't want to have anything to do with His church."

This negative sentiment about the community of believers is catching like wild-fire across the Christian landscape. One study reports, "While spirituality is flourishing, fewer people affiliate themselves with a particular denomination or religion. There is also a new phenomenon taking place in Christendom, it is called the 'Dones'. Researchers say roughly 30 million former churchgoers still maintain their faith, but they are no longer following Jesus in traditional church settings."

I once heard a pastor say this akin to a person saying to

you, "Dude, I really like hanging out with you, I think you are really cool, it is your wife I can't stand! Just don't bring her along." If you were a creepy husband this probably wouldn't bother you at all. But what if you really loved and admired your wife? How would this sound to you?

Did you know Jesus really loves his wife? He died for her. It even says in Ephesians 3:8-11 that he has a grand purpose for her, "to bring to light for everyone what is the plan of the mystery hidden for ages in God who created all things, so that through the church the manifold wisdom of God might now be made known to the rulers and authorities in the heavenly places. This was according to the eternal purpose that he has realized in Christ Jesus our Lord, in whom we have boldness and access with confidence through our faith in him."

Why then do people leave the community of believers and go out on their own? What is wrong with Jesus' bride? First, I do think there are some real legitimate reasons why some people grow frustrated with their community of faith. Here are a few listed:

1. People are tired of being lectured to, especially when they are all expected to think alike. This is especially true when they know they know more than their pastor.

2. People want to participate, but instead, they feel church is nothing more than entering into the same ole' "plop, pray and pay" routine.

3. People are genuinely tired of top-down authoritarian control and sin-management.

4. Church seems more about maintaining a rigid tradition than fostering a real relationship with God.

While these issues can bother and frustrate the average attendee, it doesn't give validation to a person's desire to abandon the church of Christ altogether, There is much written in the New Testament about forgiving, persevering and loving one another. And isn't love to be "patient and kind?" No, love is now interpreted as being set free to do whatever your heart desires. If the church isn't meeting your needs ask yourself, "Do I really love people? Have I been a change agent of grace or a critic? What does it mean to "treat one another better than yourself?" This brings me to some possible hidden and destructive reasons why I think people quit on God's bride; I offer two assessments:

1. People don't like to get involved in the messiness of other people and their problems.

2. Consumerism: People like their weekends, it is when they can finally get away and do what they want, the church just doesn't measure up in thrill, excitement and pleasure as my other options do.

In my study of Luke 2:39-52 for this Sunday's message, I find a 12-year-old boy who submitted to the customs and rules of a very traditional and rigid religious culture. It didn't make him bitter or feel mistreated. But rather he loved to be in the presence of the boring old teachers of God—and he grew in favor with others. And let me tell you, this boy was brilliant. He definitely knew more than even his mom and dad, and yet he didn't act aloof like the "cool and smart hipster people" of our day do. He obeyed joyfully.

What if Jesus quit on his disciples and community because they were just so ... backward? What if he was simply "done" with the non-sense of loving little, messy people? What if he decided to go back home to heaven because he was tired of the hassle of dealing with humanity? Or he could have made his own planet to go fly-fishing on?

If Jesus would have said adios to us the truth would be stark, "We would all die in our sin."

Stop Abusing the Blind! (On Justification)

Written May 17, 2016

"What did he do to you? How did he open your eyes?" He answered them, "I have told you already, and you would not listen. Why do you want to hear it again? Do you also want to become his disciples?" And they reviled him, saying, "You are his disciple, but we are disciples of Moses."

(John 9:26-28)

It was a horrible scene: a blind man was walking into Speedway and before he neared the entrance door he dropped his cane. As he was bending down to pick it up a bearded man in a business suit, holding a steaming 32-ounce cup of coffee, was coming out the door. He didn't see the blind man and plowed right into him, his hot coffee spilled all over his nice jacket and he started screaming:

"What the @&$?! You stupid idiot, did you see what you did to me? How could a grown man be such a fool? You were stooped down right in front of the store? What are you thinking? You piece of trash." He then gave the blind man a final shove as he crashed down in a heap hitting the hard pavement.

The man didn't stop, just huffed away into his fancy car, squealed his tires and sped off raising the bird for one last vulgar goodbye while the poor man was left lying on the ground. Two people came rushing to give the blind man assistance; one brushed him off while the other picked up his cane and directed him to the front door. The blind man's shoulder was clearly hurt...and I am sure his ego was bruised as well.

Tell me, was the blind man at fault?

Of course not. In fact, the businessman was the real jerk in this situation. If he didn't react so quickly he might have seen that the poor guy had sight impairment and hopefully he would have extended him some grace. But no, he just assumed the man was acting foolishly on purpose. Everybody should know that a blind man can't be expected to see - and to demand for him to act as a man who can see is flat out wrong. I would even say it borders on abuse.

Yelling at a blind man for not seeing accomplishes nothing, it is an impossible expectation. Blindness isn't cured by a verbal demand to see. It isn't cured by anger at a person's inability, or even statements to shame. Blindness is only cured by a miraculous healing.

However, what is clearly obvious in the physical world is often completely misunderstood in the spiritual world. This is the prime reason why so many people hate religion and feel abused in the church. Blind people are expected to act like they can see. Pastors, priests, teachers and parents place huge expectations on people demanding for them to behave as if they can see (attain righteous perfection); and as much as they try, they can't nor will they ever be able to achieve it. It is impossible. They are spiritually blind.

But Jesus says in Luke 18:27, "What is impossible with man is possible with God."

The Spiritual Condition of Man (Ephesians 2:1-3)

When a person is born into this world scripture declares we all are "Spiritually Blind—dead in our transgressions and sins." 2 Corinthians 4:4 says this blindness has the effect of warping our perspective on God and his Son Jesus Christ.

Instead of seeing him as beautiful and praiseworthy (glory is the term for this), God appears to us as an adversary, our primary object of hate. Colossians 1:21 says, "We are enemies to God in our mind."

Spiritual blindness is a fact. And yet most churches expect the spiritually blind to attain righteous perfection on their own. Churches demand we yell, and with a pointed finger of disgust, say, "Love God and obey him, or else!" But most can't even see through their hatred. We act shocked when people behave sinfully, we expect our children and the world around us to naturally perform deeds of righteousness. We wrongly teach "be righteous to become righteous." No, no, no....this is like telling a blind man to see in order to see. And the more we yell and demand and heap guilt on unrighteousness people for not living righteously, the more we are acting like the bearded businessman whose coffee got spilled. I would even say much of our discussion on "works based salvation", earning God's favor through human effort and striving to be good, is spiritual abuse.

How a Blind Man Receives Sight (Romans 1:16)

So how does the impossible become possible? How does the broken soul receive miraculous healing? The GOSPEL. It is God's power spoken to awaken a dead soul. It is when his light shines to give sight to the spiritually blind man. This moment of enlightenment is what awakens a person to the goodness of God. It has a two-step mutual process:

1. God, because of his kindness and grace, is moved by the blindness of a person, and so he invites him to receive his mercy. He does this by sending the message of his kingdom. It is a message that is unlike any other. Jesus came to earth to live the perfect life you couldn't. Jesus died, on the cross, to take the wrath against sin that you couldn't. Jesus rose from the grave to prove he actually

accomplished both. (1 Corinthians 15:1-6)

2. The Blind Man, after hearing the gospel, is moved by the Spirit of God to receive it. We call this "faith" or as Martin Luther puts it, "naked trust in Christ alone." Receiving the Gospel is a lot like a sail receiving the wind, or a hungry person receiving a loaf of bread. The Gospel is the power of God that is given to you to change you...it is what helps you see. (Titus 3:2-6)

The moment these two elements interact, or converge, new life is given. The theological term for this is "Justification." When a person exercises faith in Jesus, God assigns Jesus' righteousness on his behalf. In fact, he "declares" that person righteous. Romans 5:1 says, "Therefore being justified by faith we have peace with God through Our Lord Jesus Christ."

Justification must occur if a blind man is ever going to see.

Before I was a Christian I was a drunken, Rugby playing, partying fool. I also was empty and lost. Deep down I knew I was missing something, but I didn't know what? I even went to church, but I never felt "good enough." I tried to be religious, but the more I attempted to please God the more I knew I angered him. I was exhausted, defeated and I was done trying. And I wanted nothing to do with him.

And then I heard the gospel. I really heard it and I believed it. That is all I did, believe. After that everything seemed different. God was now for me and not against me. I wanted to be a new person. I also noticed that those in the church who used to look at me critically with furrowed brow now wanted to control me. They told me, "If I was going to be a Christian I better start looking the part."

But Christianity isn't looking a part, it is seeing life

anew. It is finally having a hope and a purpose. It is wanting to live my life for the God who saved it. Justification must take place if I am going to have the spiritual ability to see, really see—what the purpose of my life is and why God is so wonderful. When you are really are able to see, you will begin to pity those who are blind, and you also get angry at those who think they can see and can't. Usually, they are the ones who tell you how to dress and what time to show up to church. I don't go to church because I have to anymore, I go because I worship Jesus there.

Justification is the first step to real Christianity. Stop getting mad at blind people. And start living and sharing the Gospel.

Yellow Submarine Living (On Imputation)

Written May 25, 2016

"Therefore, since we have been justified by faith, we have peace with God through our Lord Jesus Christ. Through him we have also obtained access by faith into this grace in which we stand."

(Romans 5:1-2)

"Into this grace"...wow, what a statement!

Christianity at its core means to be brought into something new and great; a land of joy and abundance, it is the Kingdom of the Son he Loves (Col. 1:13). It is peace. Last week we discussed how the blind man gains sight through faith. We call that Justification. This week we are going to talk about what Justification procures for us, Imputation. Entering into the real, tangible, tasty, favor of God (Psalm 34:8).

Imputation means "a new reckoning", or accounting. God no longer holds the debt we owe him over our head. He considers the payment finished, the ledger is at zero, and as a result, His favor is now directed our way. One theologian states the process of justification to imputation like this, "A judgment is called over our life, from the other side, a transcendent voice, fully independent from our subjectivity, directed de excelsis downward, a 'judgment of justification'; which means, out of his pleasure in seeing his Son in us, God himself imputes the righteousness of Christ to humans."

He goes on to say, "God is now coming toward humans

which has a connotation of something breaking through. God's breaking through brings change and renewal." Martin Luther calls it the "happy exchange." God's Word comes from outside us, breaks through our darkness and sin, shines light that brings a new type of life. "God's word re-creates; humans are set free from bondage to the powers of sin and death" (2 Corinthians 5:17).

It also means an actual transference of positional righteousness: Jesus took upon our sin, and we were given his righteousness. Where once we were in debt to God, under his wrath, living in the land of death; imputation says now that we believe we have crossed over into a new land (John 5:24) —we are now touching the actual life of God.

I like to think of it like living in a Yellow Submarine (O.K, so I like the Beatles). Our lives have been shipwrecked by sin, we are swimming out in the deep ocean of fear with death all around us. Deadly sharks are circling, jellyfish are floating, storms are blowing, waves are cresting. And then a bright and shiny yellow submarine surfaces, a hatch pops open and a man with scars on his hands says, "Hop in, it is safe in here."

Do you trust him? Do you really have any other choice? "You are dying, jump in!"

Hopping into the submarine is like justification, you are now "In Christ"—He is our immediate deliverance, He is salvation from the sharks, storms and ocean swells that are bearing down upon us. Once you climb in, the Captain of the submarine welcomes you aboard and shows you all around. It is an amazing vessel: all the food you can eat, cozy temperature control, your own plush cot to sleep on, and a Captain whose company contains "pleasures at his right hand" (Psalm 16:11) for the whole trip. You are safe.

When you believe in Jesus, you have hopped "Into this Grace" in which you now stand, or dwell. It is real. Life becomes bigger and brighter. God's favor is like a summer breeze, refreshing and invigorating the soul.

Imputation is not earned, it is given. The submarine is something outside of you, you did not build it, it came to you when you were sinking and swallowing salt-water. The hatch was opened and all you did was enter by acceptance of the invitation of the Captain with the scarred hands. Who are we to boast? Imputation is not co-operative as some Christian sects teach, I don't rescue myself; it breaks through the violent and threatening waves in a moment to change your life forever!

I must say, imputation is rarely talked about. But it is this concept that makes Christianity real and life-giving. It is more than a concept, it is the way things really are. I will never understand God until I touch God through faith. I will never taste God until I trust God. I will never enjoy God until I rest in his strength.

Stop all this nonsense about needing proof, or answering all my doubts sufficiently...Christianity has come to rescue you, not satisfy your curiosity. If anything, the closer you are to Christ the more mysterious and wonderful he becomes.

One more thing: Muhammad doesn't have a submarine, Buddha doesn't have a submarine, and most Atheists think hoping for a sub is silly and they act like they are just fine treading water in this dangerous and unforgiving sea. And then you have those people who drank too much of the salt water of sin, who think they are doing just fine as they swim with the sharks and ignore the storms thrashing them and their families.

The hatch is NOW open, the Captain is beckoning you, will you enter?

A MAN LIKE NONE OTHER

"The Son is the radiance of God's glory and the exact representation of his being."

—Hebrews 1:3

God is a person, God is a person, God is a person!

It was my first class in seminary, before we opened up a book or took any notes my teacher stood in front of class and let us know that "God is a person." That simple little statement has never left me—but I am afraid it has left a lot of Christians.

When we lose Jesus we lose everything. Paul says, "Formerly, when you did not know God, you were slaves to those who by nature are not gods. But now that you know God—or rather are known by God– how is it that you are turning back to those weak and miserable forces? Do you wish to be enslaved by them all over again? You are observing special days and months and seasons and years."

Don't you see, when you lose the person of Jesus you turn to religious practices and moral behavior modification practices. Relationship snaps back to rituals. But God is a person, and he wants to know and be known by you.

That is what I am hoping happens in this last section, you drop the religious pretension and you come to the person. I am calling for a spiritual glasnost! Open your eyes and see the beauty of Jesus again.

"Very truly I tell you, before Abraham was born, I am!"
(John 8:58)

Light Bulb & Paper Bag (John 1:14)

Written February 14, 2014

I'll admit it, singing old hymns can be like wrestling with your brother: they sure do bring back lots of familiar memories, but after a while they can wear you out singing them. Occasionally, however, there are those hymns that can still stir the fire in your soul—easy to belt out & packed with powerful lyrics. One of those hymns for me is the song, "And Can it Be" by Charles Wesley. I love how Charles expresses the poetry of redemption in his lyrics, but there is one line in stanza three that can be rather confusing:

> *He left His Father's throne above,*
>
> *So free, so infinite His grace;*
>
> *Emptied Himself of all but love*

Emptied himself? What does that mean? Is love the only divine quality he allowed the world to see concerning his Godhood; because being able to read minds, open blind eyes and heal a woman with an issue of blood was quite spectacular (Aren't those things only God can do)?

Well, this Sunday in our John study we are going to be examining John's declaration, "The Word became Flesh." Scholars use a lot of fancy names to explain and describe this, with the chief among them being the "Incarnation." Incarnation means God becoming flesh, the Nicene Creed states it like this, "For us men, and our salvation he came down from heaven; by the power of the Holy Spirit he was born of the Virgin Mary, and was MADE MAN." Think about that a second...How can the Creator of the universe clothe himself in human skin? And when he took on humanity did that change his basic essence as God, because as scripture teaches, "God is immutable, he does not change"?

Again, scholars have come to the rescue and have given us a word derived from the original Greek language, and called Jesus' condescension to earth the "Kenosis Theory." Kenosis means to empty; Jesus emptied himself of the attributes of divinity, and that is why Charles Wesley wrote his lyrics. But this doesn't quite explain the actual reality of what happened at the incarnation and how Jesus lived his human life on earth. To expand the meaning another word to use is "veiled." Look at it like this...

THE KENOSIS THEORY

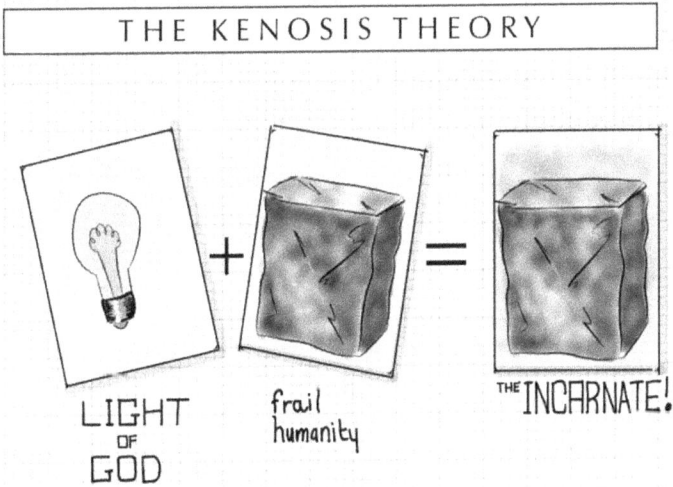

LIGHT OF GOD   +   frail humanity   =   THE INCARNATE!

The light represents the co-equal divine essence of the Son of God, and the paper bag represents the human body he was willing to take on, or like a pull-over to veil his divinity.

163

Veiling suggests that he never gave up his full power, he only covered it with true humanity. And by the words "true humanity" it means Jesus became like us in every way, he felt the fragility of the human experience fully, just as we do: all the way from a babbling baby, an awkward teen, to a full-grown man. Jesus, the Son of God, understands!

As you get ready for Sunday's sermon, I have listed some verses for you to study and meditate on:

1. Philippians 2:5-7—"What did Jesus give up to become a man?"

2. Hebrews 2:14-18—"How much of a man did Jesus become?"

One last thing: The incarnation and Kenosis haven't stopped; God's desire is to keep putting on human flesh by veiling himself in the lives of modern day people. And he wants to do this miracle through you (Galatians 1:15-16)!

The question is, will you let him?

Getting it Right: Knowing Jesus Correctly as He was, is the Key to Worshiping Him as He is

Written February 3, 2016

"With this in mind, since I myself have carefully investigated everything from the beginning, I too decided to write an orderly account for you, most excellent Theophilus, so that you may know the certainty of the things you have been taught."

(Luke 1:3-4)

Who really was Jesus?

Are you sure you know what he was like, how he lived, what he really taught? Researchers tell us that the way people view Jesus often has more to do with their personal background and experience than any other factor. If a person was raised in a white capitalist home, Jesus is seen as an enterprising entrepreneur that has come to bring you "Your Best Life Now." If a person was raised in poverty, Jesus is seen as the valiant revolutionary who has come to topple Wall Street; and like a modern day Robin Hood, deliver the money of the rich into the hands of the poor. To the atheist, Jesus never really claimed to be God; it was his zealous power-hungry followers that wanted the world to see him as more than just a mere man. (I often wonder how some critics of Christianity could think his disciples wanted power when thousands of the first century Christians were martyred and made sport of in the Roman Coliseum for what they believed?)

This is why many religious cynics say Jesus looks more like the image you find staring back at you from the mirror than a man who actually walked the dusty Middle Eastern roads 2,000 years ago. As a result, some of our more learned historians and progressive theologians have declared that knowing the real Jesus is virtually an impossible task. In the early 1800s a man by the name of David Strauss began to doubt what we have traditionally been taught about Jesus by starting a major scholastic movement called "The Quest for the Historical Jesus." Strauss began his study by rejecting all supernatural events that involved Jesus and claimed they were nothing but fictional elaborations. He viewed the miraculous accounts of Jesus' life in the gospels in "terms of myths which had arisen as a result of the community's imagination as it retold stories and represented natural events as miracles."

Over the years famous men like Albert Schweitzer and Rudolf Bultmann joined in the search for trying to understand Jesus as he was. Bultmann was a tremendously influential professor of theology at Tübingen, Germany in the early 1900's. He came to the conclusion that not much could really be known about the historical Jesus. For him, trying to find Jesus was a relatively pointless endeavor. In fact, if you want to know Jesus at all, he taught that you needed to have an existential encounter, a mystical spiritual moment, with the word of God.

Other brilliant liberal men followed in this scholarly deconstruction of Christ, with the latest being John Dominic Crossan, a former Roman Catholic priest and co-founder of the Jesus Seminar. Joining with other revisionist scholars Crossan concluded, "that many authors writing about the life of Jesus will "do autobiography and call it biography." In other words, for the present day, God seeker, real "knowing" of Jesus is nothing more than religious make-believe.

If that is the case, then tell me, who are we singing to on Sunday?

Well, for many progressive pastors like Kent Dobson, the former minister of Mars Hill Church in Grand Rapids, they are not too sure what to believe anymore. According to The Grand Rapids Press, Kent, "told the congregants that he has never felt right serving in the role of pastor because he has always been 'drawn to the edges of religion and faith and God.' He has even stated a few times that he doesn't know 'what we mean by God any more?'"

But into this fog of modern scholarship, the ancient gospel writer Luke boldly and unapologetically declares, "I have decided to write an orderly account...so you may know the certainty of things." He knew that Jesus existed, and he knew actual men and women who personally saw and heard the real Jesus walk and talk. As one very solid Christian historian, Craig Keener, writes, "Luke not only spent a lot of time with Paul in Judea, but he probably spent most of his interim in Caesarea, which afforded him the opportunity to become more 'fully acquainted' with reports about Christ's actual life." He goes on to say, that Luke had "impeccable credentials" for writing reliably about Jesus.

Not only that, but Keener goes on to say that the first-hand accounts of Jesus during Luke's day were widespread: "...hence what Luke reports was already in wide circulation at the time of his writing, probably within the lifetime of some who had known Jesus' public ministry." That should both humble the modern scholar and give confidence to the Christian reader of Luke. Because as Keener says, "whatever their (ancient writers like Luke) human biases, they were in a better historical position to evaluate matters of their day than we are today."

Luke declares that "what Jesus did was not done in a corner," (Acts 26:26) and that "Jesus of Nazareth was a man accredited by God to you by miracles, wonders and signs, which God did among you through him, as you yourselves know." (Acts 2:22). I think Luke has more reason to be believed than Strauss, Bultman or Crossan...don't you?

I wonder what people will say about me 2,000 years from now? They can read letters from my wife, kids, parents and friends or they can do extensive research on what white, male Baptist preachers were like back in the 21st century America. I can hear a haughty professor from some Ivy League school of Divinity wearing a tweed jacket saying about me:

"Well, I have done some thorough research of Reverend Christopher Weeks and his day. I know for a fact that this man was both a Caucasian and a Baptist preacher. From those two aspects alone we can extrapolate what manner of man he was. Clearly we can say that he probably was an adherent of the small but vitriolic fundamentalist sect: a group that was categorized by separatism, highly antagonistic to the culture around them, constantly participated in the degradation of women, prone to preach hellfire and damnation and a man who was apt to "cling to his guns," wore white shirts and ties and often went unhinged on his anti-alcoholic rants. We have concluded Reverend Weeks was a man who was out of touch with the community around him."

Now if you would read my correspondence to those whom I love, they know that I am anything but a hard-core fundamentalist. Actually, I am a strange and complicated man. At times I don't even understand myself! Ties make me break out in hives, I love and respect women (in truth my mom is the smartest person I know), I try to preach grace, and I barely know how to fire a squirt gun.

The point being, you don't learn about a man by the culture he lived in, but you learn about a man by the people who knew and loved him. If you disagree, answer me one thing: Are you exactly like your brothers and sisters? Just because you were raised in the same home does not make you alike.

One Israeli scholar writes, "The early Christian accounts about Jesus are not as untrustworthy as scholars today often think. The first three Gospels not only present a reasonably faithful picture of Jesus as a Jew in his own time but portray him quite plausibly as a Jewish miracle-worker and preacher," rather than some made up object of the church's proclamation. C.S. Lewis quips, "The earliest converts were converted by a single historical fact (the Resurrection) and a single theological doctrine (the Redemption) operating on a sense of sin they already had." They didn't need some highly accredited scholar's assurance to prove the historical accuracy of Christ.

I believe if we lose the scripture's account of Jesus, we will lose Jesus himself. In order to worship a Jesus that isn't make-believe, let's stick to what has been revealed to us through the Holy Scriptures.

It is here we become certain!

"UNTIL": God's Way to Enter His Wonder

Written February 12, 2016

"But when you pray, go into your room and shut the door and pray to your Father who is in secret. And your Father who sees in secret will reward you."

(Matthew 6:6)

In my sophomore & junior year of college I decided to sign up for some very tough "electives": General classes that were outside of my business marketing major but still applied to my overall credits. I wanted to choose some courses to help me be a more intellectual and well-rounded student. After perusing the different options that were offered, I picked three that sounded especially hard: Camping, Canoeing and Scuba Diving. (And to think my parents only thought I goofed around at school?)

In all seriousness, I chose Camping and Canoeing because they were easy "A's"; not only did they offer loads of outdoor time with my friends, but they required "zero" mental strain and labor. So wanting to take one more breeze class, I signed up for Scuba Diving. After the first day of class, I came to a quick realization that this was going to be a different sort of animal altogether. It was to push me to my limits on three personal levels:

1. Physically it demanded each student to be in great swimming shape. We had to be able to swim 20

laps across the pool and then tread water for 30 minutes before we could even touch the actual scuba equipment. Many students dropped the class once they heard that this was a mandatory requirement to pass.

2. Mentally you had to learn a lot about the human body's circulatory and respiratory system. There are two very real risks when you go diving in deep water: Decompression Sickness, otherwise known as the "The Bends", and Nitrogen Narcosis. The teacher made sure we understood the extreme seriousness of these dangers before we even stuck one toe into the water.

3. Emotionally this class directly confronted some of your worst fears. The teacher scheduled us to dive in some flooded quarries found in Northern Ohio, where they went 150 feet down into inky black, ice-cold waters. I assure you, 150 feet is really deep and it can feel terribly claustrophobic. As we began to dive these waters I often had to trade partners because after reaching certain depths some students would panic and refuse to go any deeper. I must tell you...I loved this class and I really came to enjoy Scuba Diving. I would tell other students about my diving experiences and then they would ask me, "Why would anyone choose to subject themselves to the silent prison of such cold black water, not knowing which way was up, or facing the possibility of encountering an angry catfish, a curious nibbling carp or being chased by the dreaded shrieking eels?" (They watched way too much Princess Bride.)

My answer was simple, "It is a strange thrill when you can survive in a place that normally would kill you." There is a wonder about it. Scuba brought me into the mystery of new sights and strange sounds. I was able to experience things I never had before and saw things relatively few ever did.

One of the first times we put on our Scuba equipment, our teacher put us under a very curious test. He gave us 15 minutes to get familiar with breathing out of a regulator: You would stand in the pool up to your waist, put the regulator into your mouth, and then stick your head under the water while breathing in and out like Darth Vader. It took some practice, but soon we all were comfortable with breathing in the water.

Next, he then had our class go sit with our full equipment on at the bottom of a 15-foot pool. There we sat. Enjoying the experience of breathing freely under water. Out of nowhere, our teacher came swimming down to the bottom with a pair of Scuba fins and proceeded to pull our regulators out of our mouths. Many in the class panicked and quickly swam to the surface. A few of us tried to stay at the bottom to prove we could survive his little test. The only problem was that we couldn't breath—that is . . .

UNTIL . . .

UNTIL . . .

UNTIL . . .

until we stopped panicking, reached back, grabbed our regulators, placed them in our mouths and started breathing the slow "in and out" Vader pattern again. There we sat...breathing freely, safe and sound, happy that we passed this test.

The key to our survival was experiencing the moment of "Until."

This is when the human mind realizes two things: Our desperate "need" and the "solution" that is offered to meet that need. "Until" is what made the Scuba experience wonderful.

"Great story, but...seriously, what does this have to do with anything?" Stick with me and you will see. To help explain what I am getting at I ask you to turn to Psalm 73 and read the first 16 verses. I know most of you won't do this because cracking open your bible is a rare endeavor...so let me explain what it says.

In the first 16 verses, the writer of Psalm 73 is both depressed & distressed. He is trying to be true to God but his life is falling apart. As he looks around, people who have no regard for the things of God seem to be doing fine, and this really ticks him off. So much so, he asks himself in verse 13, "What's the use? Why be clean, why be pure, why be a good religious guy?" Now it gets exciting, and verse 17 is the key verse to the whole psalm:

"*Until* I went into the sanctuary of God; then I discerned their end."

The Psalmist was in despair, "Until." It is just like me in Scuba class, I could not breathe underwater "Until." It is the way God designed reality. He brings us to the brink of despair so we will reach out for him through the "Until." (see Romans 11:32) It is that place of solitude, silence, alone where we invite the presence of God to change our perspective, circumstances and our life.

Jesus calls this moment of "Until" the prayer closet, the secret place, a person's own personal sanctuary. And in the prayer closet, he tells us to "Ask, Seek, and Knock" (Matthew 7:7-8). In Luke 1:5-25, the story of Zechariah and Elizabeth, all their dreams to have a child of their own were smashed, that is "Until" Zechariah went into the Holy Place and offered incense, the visible sign of prayer.

When I was in Scuba class, I couldn't breath underwater "until" I reached for the regulator. The regulator brought "oxygen" down to my lungs so I could survive in 150 feet of the icy dark deep. Often my life is too much for me, "until" I enter the secret place, and my prayer invites the "Actual Presence of God" to come down into my strange world of depression and despair. Oxygen is the physical stuff of the world above water; God's presence brings to me the Spiritual stuff of heaven. God is just as real and far more powerful and effective than oxygen.

I want to take this a step further: Just as Scuba diving brought me into "the mystery of new sights and strange sounds. I was able to experience things I never had before and saw things relatively few ever did," this is even more true with prayer. Wonder is so rare in the church because prayer is so rare. Rarely are we desperate, rarely do we reach the point of "Until."

The Physics of God

Written April 26, 2016

It is getting to the end of the school year, and so all of you students of Theology should be ready for the final exam. Hopefully, you have studied up so you can answer the final question. It is worth 100% of the grade for the class. This is for all the marbles....

FINAL QUESTION: If Johnny wants to make it to heaven with absolute certainty, which formula should he use to get there?

(A) F = J + W

(B) F + W = J

(F - Faith, W - Work, J - Justification —If you answered (A) you pass. If (B), we need to talk.)

While reading "Are We Together" by R. C. Sproul*, I was brought back to the wonder and exhilaration I first felt when I finally discovered the "true gospel" that is taught clearly in the Bible. You see, for 23 years I was unsure of what God wanted from me. Different people told me different things, the nuns told me one thing, the priests another, and both groups didn't often see things quite like my grandparents and parents did. I realized at the age of 18, nobody really knew if they were right or wrong!

Climbing the stairway to heaven seemed like a crap-shoot.

As I look back on it now, the reason why there was such confusion on the topic of salvation is because they were all using the wrong formula: answer (B). As much as you may try, the wrong formula will never give you a correct answer—every physics student knows this. In the same way, people think they can ignore the importance of correct doctrine, but precision of thought and language is always necessary if you are going to come to the right answer. This is especially true when it comes to where you spend eternity. It is funny, when people build a house precision is expected. My dad would throw me a tape measure and say "measure twice and cut once." Exactness mattered. But for some strange reason, people have a terrible habit of using fuzzy math when it comes to the things of God.

So let's get precise.

THE RIGHT ANSWER:
F = J + W (Faith = Justification and Works)

"One thing I do know, that though I was blind, now I see." They said to him, "What did he do to you? How did he open your eyes?" He answered them, "I have told you already, and you would not listen. Why do you want to hear it again? Do you also want to become his disciples?" (John 9:25-27)

This formula is the "true gospel", the one that truly saves. It is fairly straightforward. On the left side of the equation, we have the only thing needed that is necessary for a person to please God (Hebrews 11:6), FAITH (F)! As the early reformers would put it, "Sola Fide", faith alone. So what exactly is faith? Is it wishing something will come true or hoping God is who he says he is? No, both of those ideas fall short of the true, solid, biblical definition of faith. Faith is "receiving and resting on Christ and his righteousness and his righteousness alone." I can't add a single thing to what he already did—he drank the cup of wrath for all of us when he died on the cross (Matthew 26:42) and he rose again to prove

God was fully pleased. Faith trusts that his death and resurrection was a complete payment on my behalf. This is something none of us could ever do...and he did it out of love for us!

Now the right side of the equation is where it gets interesting. The first element after a man exercises faith is called "Justification" (J). This term means, "Declared righteous by God himself." You see when I receive Christ, I receive his life. This is called imputation; all that Jesus has accomplished is "credited" to me. So if I receive the gospel by faith, God forever sees his Son in me (2 Corinthians 5:21). R.C. Sproul says this kind of justification is called "synthetic justification", something outside of me was added to my life, an alien righteousness. I was blind, and Jesus had to give me sight that was not originally mine.

And this imputation is both real and powerful.

So powerful it will produce fruit, which is signified by the final variable, "W". I will start working, not to earn, gain or secure a standing. Synthetic justification says I already have it (Romans 5:1), but I work because the life of Christ is now alive in me. As James says, "Faith without works is dead" which means if I have no works I probably didn't exercise true faith in the first place. If God gives me sight, I will prove it through seeing. If God gives me his Son's imputed life, I will prove it through loving. If someone isn't working it may be because they never really exercised true faith. You can't do work in order produce work, in the same way, a blind man can't first see in order to receive sight. It must be first given to you by God. This is true salvation.

THE WRONG ANSWER:
F + W = J (Faith + Works = Justification)

"And behold, a man came up to him, saying, 'Teacher,

what good deed must I do to have eternal life?' And he said to him, 'Why do you ask me about what is good? There is only one who is good. If you would enter life, keep the commandments.'...The young man said to him, 'All these I have kept. What do I still lack?' Jesus said to him, 'If you would be perfect, go, sell what you possess and give to the poor, and you will have treasure in heaven; and come, follow me.'" (Matthew 19:16-17; 20-21)

This formula is the "tricky and tiring gospel" because it sounds so right, and yet it is oh so wrong and exhausting. It sounds so right because the variables seem the same, but they do not mean the same thing. Faith (F) again is used in the equation, but if you notice, it is not complete. It isn't enough, you need to help it out by adding Work (W). This faith is not "imputed" it is "infused". Infused faith is not complete faith. It is like jump-starting a car, Jesus' death on the cross started us out on the path to righteousness, but it isn't enough to fully get to the destination. It is up to us and our efforts to continue working toward it the rest of the way, that is why "W" needs to be added to it.

What kind of work needs to be done? This is the problem, it depends on who you ask. I know priests who said you need to do penance, others said you need simple sincerity, I had nuns that said to pray to Mary, and then you have the regular guy that said you just had to be baptized as an infant. Standards were always shifting and certainty was an impossibility.

The number one phrase that described the work that was needed was "Be Good." But what does it even mean to be good? Who decides on the correct standard of goodness? If it is a cool priest or liberal nun, you just need to be a liberal democrat and give a lot of money to the poor. If it is your parents who decide what the standard is, it is pretty easy, just be yourself. But in the verse I quoted earlier, Jesus said, "Be perfect."

Wait a minute? Did you say perfection? In Theological terms, perfection is sinlessness. Can a person be perfect? Did you know Mother Teresa wasn't even perfect? Just read Romans 3:11-23 and you will soon realize no one is perfect. And that is the problem. To get to the "J" in our formula you need to do enough "W" to make the "F" sufficient. And that depends on an imperfect person (you), to achieve perfection (impossible)!

Oh yeah, one more important thing about this formula: The "J" is still representing justification, but it is not "synthetic justification" but rather "analytical justification." That means when all's said and done, God analyzes a person and their work to see if they are truly righteous. But remember, perfection is the standard God is obligated to use (Habakkuk 1:13), and none of us has it in us. Do you see the problem?

THE TRACK MEET:

There are two track meets to heaven. The first one is the biblical race: The gun goes off to begin the race when a person believes in Christ alone. As they run, sometimes they fall, but they can still get up because they are already on the team....they will never be kicked off. The finish line is the moment of death, it is at that time when a person will be granted glorification, the likeness of Christ forever.

The second one is the religious race: The gun goes off when a person is born, but you never quite know when they make the team. If a person falls during the race, it better not be a fall that is so bad it will get them disqualified. But in this race, every fall is that bad! In fact, the whole race is trying to achieve perfection so you will finally make the team. When they get to the finish line, it is then that their race is judged, and you never know the outcome because you never know if you did enough. The truth is, no one ever runs the perfect race, so in this race, no one ever does enough. That is why it is so exhausting…

Only one person has run the perfect race, Jesus, and when a person believes, God attributes Jesus' race to them. That is why you will only hear cheering from the first race, it begins at the beginning of the race and never stops all through eternity! Which answer did you choose, and which race are you running?

Was Jesus Ever Caught Off Guard?
(God Dazed & Confused)

Written June 17, 2016

Could Jesus be hoodwinked? Is he ever perplexed, with furrowed brow, wringing hands, as he watches the world turn? And I am not talking about your grandma's favorite Soap Opera. My main query is wondering whether or not if God is ever dazed and confused or caught off guard when considering the actions of the human race?

Personally, I think he is.

But how can this be? God is Sovereign, he knows and sees all things. According to Isaiah 46:10 he is the one who "declared the end from the beginning." So, theoretically speaking, he can never be caught off guard. Right?

Some argue that God figures things out as he goes along. There is a teaching out there that says he is often surprised at some of reality's unforeseen twists and turns—and he certainly is perplexed at our quirky human foibles. For instance, in the last 20 years, some progressive thinkers have implemented a curious new interpretive schematic called the "Redemptive Hermeneutic" when trying to understand the Bible. The Redemptive Hermeneutic teaches that "the moral commands of the New Testament do not always represent a perfect or final moral system for Christians." They are rather a pointer that "provides the direction toward an ultimate destination, but its literal, isolated words are not always the destination itself."

In other words, at the time the Bible was written, God was still in the dark about a number of complex ethical issues.

You could say, he was still working out his redemptive theology, along with our cooperation and insights, and it has taken the last 2,000 years for both of us together to come to the brighter light of interpretative truth.

Two issues that these left-leaning cultural critics point at to illustrate God's growth in understanding are "slavery" and "consensual homosexual unions." The person who first presented this idea was the writer William Webb. He believes "our contemporary culture" has a better ethic than what is found in the words of the Bible. The Bible at the time of it's writing wasn't fully complete. God was still in process.

And logically speaking, a God in process is not a God fully in the know.

So when it comes to slavery, Webb says the bible at the time of the writing "approved of slavery with many abuses." But now, after fighting all our civil rights battles, "our culture is much closer to an ultimate ethic than it is to the unrealized ethic reflected in the isolated words of the Bible" So God, along with us, is still learning. And if God is learning, he can be caught off guard.

This approach can also be taken when it comes to supporting homosexual unions. As one pro-gay writer states, "The Bible routinely, clearly, and strongly classifies all sex acts outside of the bonds of marriage as sinful. But, because when the Bible was written there was no concept of gay people—let alone, then, of gay marriage—the Bible does not, and could not, address the sinfulness of homosexual acts within the context of marriage." In other words, God was caught off guard again. He never considered the idea of a pure and loving homosexual relationship. It took the brilliant minds of the people living in the 21st century to bring to light the concept of noble 'gayness'.

In both cases, slavery and homosexuality, supporters of The Redemptive Hermeneutic want us to believe God was caught off guard. Or at least they want us to be gullible enough to accept the extremely arrogant idea that he is now pleasantly surprised with the results of our ever-enlightened civility. Human history became his laboratory to help him flesh out his redemptive ethics and bring clarity to the new societal changes that he wasn't able to foresee when he first had men pen the bible. God needed us to help him.

How silly. How blasphemous.

God wrote a perfect and flawless bible, as Proverbs 30:5-6 says, "Every word of God proves true; he is a shield to those who take refuge in him. Do not add to his words, lest he rebuke you and you be found a liar." To say he didn't give to us a fully complete canon is both patently offensive, and it paints the Holy Spirit's work of inspiration as incomplete. The truth is God is more than clear about the sin of stealing humans and selling them as slaves (Exodus 21:16, 1 Timothy 1:10), and he is equally straightforward about the sin of homosexuality (Romans 1:26-27). God was not caught of guard, nor was he waiting for us to evolve to a new state of understanding. No, this teaching is nothing more than a bunch of ignorant fools casting God in the role of an idiot.

And God is no idiot, and his Bible is infallible and true. However, I still think there is one thing that does have him confused...or at least it causes him untold frustration. This one thing is found in Luke 6:46...

"Why do you call me, 'Lord, Lord,' and do not do what I say?"

God is perplexed when human beings claim Christ as Lord, and yet treat him as chopped liver. You may wonder what is the big deal, we are giving him props, aren't we? Isn't that really all that God wants? Our praise? When we call him Lord we are doing exactly what he told us to do. He loves it when we sing. He loves it when we pack our churches, pump up the volume and shout our lungs out. Doesn't he?

Aren't we doing his will when we find the best looking people with the best voices leading "sold out" believers in praise? Why do we think singing and crying is being "sold out"? We are such silly people. Anyone can sing. Anyone can cry. Few obey.

Let's slow it down a second: What do we mean when we call Jesus Lord? I'm not sure we know what we mean, but I know what God thinks it should mean. And listen closely, it will rock your world:

"A son honors his father, and a servant his master. If then I am a father, where is my honor? And if I am a master, where is my fear? says the Lord of hosts to you, O priests, who despise my name...Oh that there were one among you who would shut the doors, that you might not kindle fire on my altar in vain! I have no pleasure in you, says the Lord of hosts, and I will not accept an offering from your hand. For from the rising of the sun to its setting my name will be great among the nations, and in every place incense will be offered to my name, and a pure offering. For my name will be great among the nations, says the Lord of hosts...Cursed be the cheat who has a male in his flock, and vows it, and yet sacrifices to the Lord what is blemished. For I am a great King, says the Lord of hosts, and my name will be feared among the nations." (Mal. 1:6, 10-11, 14)

Did you catch that? When you call Jesus Lord you are saying he is "Great!" You believe "He is to be feared." And yet most of us pay him only lip service. God can melt mountains, and tear open skies! And yet we demand he serve us!

How dare we. How dare we demand Him to let us sleep with whoever we want, how dare we demand Him to look past our sick deeds of lust. How dare we pervert His word to suit our needs and act as if He is the one who sanctioned it!!! And do you know what is even worse than all that? When we don't listen to him but presume upon him to listen to our prayers and expect him to obey us.

Is Jesus God? Is He a great Lord?

If He is, then...do what He says.

Let Jesus Christ Be...Blamed?

Written August 18, 2016

"Let no one say when he is tempted, "I am being tempted by God," for God cannot be tempted with evil, and he himself tempts no one."

(James 1:13)

Here is a question that was recently asked me, "If God is good, why does he allow people to become addicted?" Is God to be held responsible for the world that is currently in chaos? Should Jesus Christ be blamed, because he is currently sitting on his Father's throne? This is a tough, tough question; and it is a question that has been asked by every generation, in every time, and I believe in every human heart that has ever lived. Theologians call this the question of "Theodicy":

- **If God is good, why did he create Satan?**
- **If God is good, why do innocent people suffer?**
- **If God is good, why do babies die?**
- **If God is good, why do the scriptures threaten hell?**
- **If God is good, why do I hurt so much?**

Evil and a good all-powerful God seem mutually exclusive? I recently read an interesting twist on this question,

"It appears to be part of human nature to cry out, 'Why has

this happened to me?' when tragedy or suffering hits life, but hardly ever to ask, 'What have we done to deserve this?' when life is blessed with health or prosperity. Some suggest that the problem of evil can be addressed only when we ask the problem of good."

This question of evil will never go away. It will always be a part of the human experience, it is what beckons us to reach out to God in faith.

But have you ever looked at evil from God's point of view? He is more perplexed and frustrated about it than you are. Let me help you see the world from his perspective.

THE BEST POSSIBLE CHOICE

God could have created the world any way he wanted, but being perfect he must choose the best possible world for all and that world includes "choice." Love cannot be compelled, and good infers bad. As Augustine said, "Evil exists only in good; our Universe enjoys light and shade, and life and death...What is more beautiful than a fire? What is more useful than heat and comfort?... Yet nothing can cause more distress than the burns inflicted by fire."

Love is hot, and God wants us to love him, it is the basis of worship - but that must mean rejection is a possibility. If you don't believe me, try this out sometime; Tell your wife you love her because you have no other choice...

"Honey, why did you buy me flowers?"

Because I am supposed to.

"Did you want to?"

It doesn't matter - I had to.

Yuck! That is not love, it is a horror movie; "Invasion of the Body Snatchers." So in order for love to be love, it must include choice.

REJECTING THE BEST

Now when it comes to loving God, there is a lot at stake. If I reject loving the girl across the room, it doesn't necessarily cost me much because she is a finite human being. But God is infinite in love, goodness, and righteousness in himself. He is the source of all life, and when I reject him I am rejecting what is best for me.

When I reject the source of all that is good, what is left? Evil. When I reject light, what is left? Darkness. When I reject love, "God is love", what is left? Indifference, malice, hatred, envy, jealousy, rage.

A PEAK INTO THE HEART OF GOD

Jeremiah 2 is one of the saddest and most tragic windows into the heart of God. In verses 2-3 God pictures Israel, his people, as a beautiful bride that he was madly in love with. Like a pair of honeymooners, God was intoxicated with the beauty of his young bride. And if anybody tried to take his beloved away, "they incurred guilt; disaster came upon them." In other words, don't mess with God's woman!

But in verse 5, something worse than his bride being taken away happened. The bride herself didn't want to be married anymore. God asked the question to Israel, "What wrong did your fathers find in me that they went far from me?"

God is asking his people, "What is wrong with me that you want to leave me?" Do you hear his pain? Do you feel the brokenness of his heart? God, the "perfection of beauty" (Psalm 50:2), was rejected for another lover. Romans 1:21-22 says, "Although they knew God...they exchanged his glory (heavy beauty) for images resembling mortal man and birds and animals and creeping things."

They traded God for garbage. We trade God for garbage.

I can remember after dating my wife for a while I met a few of her past boyfriends. Compared to me, they were schmucks and I told her so. Hey, I am not being harsh, I was in love with her—I still am, and I still feel the same way. Compared to me they are schmucks. I know what is best for her, so even the suggestion of her going back to those silly boys makes me crazy. This is what God is saying in Jeremiah 2. Listen to verse 12,

"Be appalled, O heavens, at this; be shocked, be utterly desolate...for my people have committed two evils (the true theodicy): they have forsaken me, the fountain of living waters, and hewed out cisterns for themselves, broken cisterns that can hold no water."

In other words, they already had the best, "living waters", and traded it for stagnant old rainwater that leaked out of the cistern. Stupid, stupid, sad, so sad.

WHAT AN APPLE IS ASKING

God wants to be loved, that's all. And that is what worship means, "Is he worth it?" This is why he placed a tree called "the knowledge of good and evil" in the middle of the Garden of Eden. It was the way Adam showed his choice. Is God better than a fruit that looks pleasing? Is he "worth" the sacrifice? If so, say no.

- **Is God worth being sexually pure for?**
- **Is God worth being sober for?**
- **Is God worth being kind to others for?**

If so, say no to your fleshly desires. Don't let them win. Love God by not turning to other lovers. Why? What happens if I do turn to other lovers?

Listen to Jeremiah 2:5b, "they went after worthlessness, and became worthless." As one writer has famously said,

"What you worship you become like." Listen to Romans 1:26 on this matter, "Because they exchanged the truth of God for a lie...God gave them up (or over) to dishonorable passions." People become addicted to what they crave.

GOD IS A CHASTE LOVER

Every noble dad wants their daughter to be chaste. This means virtuous and willing to wait until the right man comes. This is one of the greatest tragedies from the sexual revolution; women now think it is cool and freeing to "put-out" like juvenile debased men do because they want to be equal. Tragically when a woman "puts-out" they are playing into the hands of the evil heart of men's lust.

Sex isn't meant to be a game, it is a sacred gift reserved for the one who protects it.

When your daughter is chaste, she ultimately finds the man who really means it when he says, "I love you." You see, those words are meant to mean something--I want what is best for you, and it isn't simply getting your body for a one night stand.

God also is waiting, hiding, longing for people to love him truly. He is far too valuable to give of himself to people who are merely paying him lip service Sunday morning. He wants people who really want him. So to find those who want to worship, he places before them a tree.

"If you love me, say 'no' to the idol."

Have you ever noticed, those who are addicted to things like sex, drugs, and perverted lifestyle choices seem to get mad at God? They are quick to blame him for their behavior. They see theodicy as his problem and not theirs. The truth is they don't like him being so specific. They want him to be tolerant, unchaste, a whore. But he is holy. And it is his holiness that makes him wholly beautiful. As Job says in

31:23,

"For fear of his splendor, I could not do such things."

THE IMPORTANCE OF THE CROSS

God still loves you even in your rebellion. So to rescue you while you are addicted to evil, he sends his Son to become evil. "Cursed is everyone who hangs upon the tree."

Where is God in your suffering? "He is hanging on the tree!"

This is his plan to rescue you. He has allowed himself to be punished for your unfaithfulness, so you can become faithful. Look at him. Is he to be blamed for evil when he willingly allowed it to kill him? He has done this for you? God has done it for you because he wants you back.

Listen to him in Jeremiah 31:33:

"This is the covenant I will make with Israel after those days, declares the Lord: I will put my law within them, and I will write it on their hearts. And I will be their God, and they shall be my people."

Why is there evil, why are people addicted, why is there suffering? Because you chose garbage over God. Don't blame Jesus, but rather, believe in him. Run to him. It is the only way to escape from yourself.

An Indestructible, Unassailable and Invincible Soul

Written September 8, 2016

"There is no fear in love, but perfect love casts out fear. For fear has to do with punishment, and whoever fears has not been perfected in love. "

(1 John 4:18)

The world is full of wounded people. Easily hurt, overwhelmed with guilt, shame, anxiety; and crippled by fear. Does this describe you?

Why are we so fragile?

Many of our lives are resting on a cracked foundation, built with the rotten wood of self. When people like us, we feel strong. But when people criticize, argue, complain or even register indifference in our presence, the world seems to crumble around our feet. Joker once asked Batman, "Why so serious?" That is the wrong question. The most telling one is, "Why so worried?"

The most commonly used description of humanity's collective state of the soul is "insecure": I am not sure I am going to make it? I am not sure I have enough in myself to make it? I just want to crawl in a hole and die. I know you have had morbid thoughts like this—because I do, all the time. Just look around you, why else are people so angry? Why do we have to micro-manage what we say to people? Why does everyone seem to be so uptight when it comes to politics, health, money, and relationships? Because fear and our own personal inability to effect change makes us all a little apprehensive.

So what is the cure? How do I obtain security? I want to have an indestructible, unassailable and invincible soul. Don't you? I know it can't be who we put in office, Hilary or Donald, it can't be a good interest rate on our investment, or people hitting the like button on my Instagram pic. So what is the solution?

Before I tell you, you must be ready to be honest with yourself. You must stop playing games and quit hiding. Stop acting like you are better than you are. Get alone where it is quiet, sit down with nothing else (no phone, Ipad, computer or TV) and ask yourself this:

"Do I 'feel' loved by God?"

I know we are not to predicate our faith on feeling, however, feeling is a crucial part of human existence. I once read your soul is like a man riding a 1,000-pound elephant. The man represents "reason", and the elephant is "emotion." Reason can only move a person so far...but once emotion gets moving, wow, you have real power to live by.

So, do you feel loved?

O.K., what do I mean by loved? I think the feeling of love includes three components: I know I am wanted, I know I am accepted, and I know that I am delighted in. Scripture says love is patient, kind, keeps no record of wrongs...but remember, we are talking about feelings. Feelings are your personal perception of another's attitude toward you. That is where it gets tricky.

There is a story about a man and woman who got married and after 40 years of marriage, the wife was fed up with her husband's lack of communication. So she demanded they get marriage counseling. The counselor asked the wife what was wrong with the marriage? She replied, "He doesn't love me."

The man said, "Sure I do. Where did you ever get that silly idea?" The wife in disgust said, "You never say 'I love you.'" And the man looked at her and flatly stated, "I said I loved you 40 years ago on the altar. If I changed my mind I would have told you."

She needed to "feel" loved. Everyone does. Especially when it comes to a God we can't see. We all need to know: Does God want me, does he accept me, and does he delight in me? How you answer and then process this will either make or break your soul. Oh sure, you can act like God's opinion doesn't matter, but when you are alone, and it is deathly quiet, you are wired to wonder, "Hmmm, how does God view me?"

And don't act like it doesn't matter. . .

As scripture says, "The fool has said in his heart there is no God." So you know he exists, and you know his opinion about you matters more than anyone else's. So, does God love you?

This morning, I really meditated on this. Even I, a pastor for 20 some odd years, need to know. I need to feel.

Instantly, this is what came flooding to my mind:

1. JESUS TOOK MY PLACE ON THE CROSS: That is how much God wants me. In order to take my place, he voluntarily chose to come down to this smelly and violent earth from heaven, and be nailed naked on a tree. He stood in for me. He clenched his teeth, shut his mouth and allowed the world to rip him apart. . . for me. No one else would ever do that for me! Especially if they really knew me—a mistake-prone myopic jerk, an enemy to his holiness, a selfish man—he wanted me, even then. He wants me now!

2. AT THE CROSS, GOD'S WRATH WAS FULLY UNLEASHED, AND COMPLETELY EXHAUSTED: The Father's anger toward me was aimed at his Son. All of it. Jesus drank the cup of wrath "down to its dregs" at the cross. In those short three hours, God emotionally unleashed all his eternal fury, "It was the will of the Lord to crush him; he has put him to grief." (Isaiah 53:10) The pounding Jesus took fully satisfied the justice of heaven. So, now, there is no more anger to unleash on me, wrath is quenched. Through Jesus, and because of his payment, when I exercise faith in him, God the Father accepts me...I belong!

3. THE RESURRECTION IS GOD'S STAMP OF DELIGHT AND APPROVAL: It is one thing to have your sins paid for, to have wrath extinguished, it is quite another to be embraced as worthy. I know a man who once told me that he knows God has to allow him in heaven because of the cross, but he isn't sure God likes him and wants him to be there. Like a member of the family that sits in the corner and everyone is good with it; this man felt like God had to love him, but he really didn't want to love him. No, no, no, when you believe, you become a valued and irreplaceable member of the family. You are the brother that everyone can't wait to see, the beloved college kid returning home for Thanksgiving. Where mom is waiting at the door, little brother is watching from the window and dad is texting wondering when you will arrive. God longs for you in the same way, because he delights in you. God likes me!

When you know you have the invincible God on your side, you can be sure you have nothing to fear. You are secure.

Here is one of the most reassuring verses ever given to the person who begins to feel loved, "He who did not spare his own Son but gave him up for us all, how will he not also with him graciously give us all things?" (Romans 8:32) Why are you worried that God, who already gave you his Son, may not give you exactly what you need this moment?

He broke the bank when he sacrificed his Son.

So why so worried? Is it because you really never believed in him in the first place? Maybe that is why you are so insecure...I would be too!

What Does the Cross Mean to Me?

Written March 27, 2018

Jesus died.

The one person who did nothing wrong paid for all of my wrongs. And there are too many to count. I should be better at so much: A husband, a father, a pastor, a brother, a son. I am all of these and I fail.

As a husband, I haven't loved my wife enough. Said the wrong things at the wrong times. Sat on the couch too much and too long. Demanded many things in simmering anger.

As a father, I have been lazy and lax. I haven't taught and trained as I should. I have gotten mad when I should have listened. I can't get the years back.

As a pastor, I definitely don't pray nearly enough. I preach at times to perform. I like to be liked.

As a brother, I don't keep in contact. I slip in, wave, hug and slip out.

As a son...the list is too long.

And then I read in Psalm 69:4 one line that stops my heart. I am overwhelmed every time I read it. It makes no sense:

"What I (Jesus) did not steal must I (Jesus) now restore?"

This is the cross. A payment for my failure. At every point I have stumbled, fell, rebelled and willfully sinned, Jesus paid for it.

It makes no sense.

Why would he do this? Why did he let me go free? I failed. I keep failing, and I always will.

The only thing I can figure is John 14:3, "I (Jesus) will

come again and will take you to myself, that where I am you may be also."

Jesus wants to be with me.

And the cross was the only way.

It makes no sense, but I accept.

CONCLUSION

Why are Russians Sad?

"The world of the fairy tale impinges on the ordinary world the way the dimension of depth impinges on the two-dimensional surface of a plane, so that there is no point on the plane-a Victorian sitting room or a Kansas farm-that can't become an entrance to it. You enter the EXTRAORDINARY by way of the ORDINARY. Something you have seen a thousand times you suddenly see as if for the first time...you do not have to go a great distance to enter it any more than you have to go a great distance to enter the world of dreams-you just have to go to sleep-or the world of memory..."

—Frederick Buechner (Telling the Truth)

I was watching a raindrop in Russia.

Framed in a cloudy backdrop of gray, a single bead of lonely water fell silently out of the sky. It traveled a short journey from the bottom of the lacy dark canopy tumbling quickly down to die on a hard surface of dry concrete. It ended quietly. No cry or whimper, just the sound of a soft pat hitting the ground. Within seconds it was swallowed by the cracks and dimples of a thirsty sidewalk.

Is that what life is like for you? A sad straight line downward? Are you just existing to exist? Is there any magic or only dull tedium?

I am not by nature a depressed person, but there are days when I wonder is that all? Is my day only the same day lived,

201

again and again, a drab existence covered in a cloud of emotional gray? Am I a Russian raindrop?

Listen to this quote by Frederick Buechner, it is aimed at preachers like me who forget the real fairy tale we are daily living in:

"The truth, reality, is what it is. It is the TV news with the sound turned on and all the other sound turned on with it-the sounds of the house, of the street outside the house, the town, the countryside, the world...The truth is all the sounds that well up within the preacher as he sits down at his desk to put his sermon together-the sounds of the bills to be paid, the children to educate, the storm windows to put up, the sounds of his own blunders and triumphs, of his lusts and memories and dreams and doubts, and one of which when you come right down to it is apt to seem more real and immediate and clamorous to him than the sound of truth as high and wild and holy.

So homiletics becomes apologetics. The preacher exchanges the fairy-tale truth that is too good to be true for a truth that...secularizes and makes rational. He adapts and makes relevant. He demythologizes and makes credible. And what remains of the fairy tale of the Gospel becomes in his hands a neutered narrative where there are few surprises."

Is the Gospel a fairy tale? Not in the sense that it is a completely made-up, make-believe story; but it is in the sense that when understood rightly it is "high, wild and holy. It is magical!" Yes, the Gospel is meant to be wild, and magical. It is meant to awaken my soul to another world that exists just beyond my sight. But to the average preacher, like me, and the average Christian, like you, the Gospel is often seen merely as an insignificant add-on to the monotony of my ho-hum daily routine. Like the Russian raindrop, my life quietly, silently, unceremoniously descends.

That isn't much of a fairy tale. In fact, that isn't even

magical. And that isn't the Gospel.

Frederick Buechner says there are three components to the fairy tale that are also true to the Gospel:

1. The hidden world is full of darkness and danger. He says that in the fairy tale there are "fierce dragons that guard the treasure, wicked fairies who show up at royal christenings, wrong turns off the path, an awful price to be paid for choosing the wrong casket or wrong door. It is a world of a dark and dangerous quest where the suitors compete for the hand of the king's daughter with death to the losers..." The Gospel has been sold differently than this. We have come to see it as something tame. A list of ideas, cold principles and irrelevant historical facts that you learn on Sunday, but is not does really contain the warp and woof of real living. The Gospel doesn't pay the bills, it adds little to help troubled relationships, it offers relatively nothing in the immediate stressful schedule of the day. But I believe if you were to actually read the Bible rightly, the Gospel is first and foremost the entrance into a real world full of darkness and danger, of beasts and creatures fully fanged. In my Proverbs study, I often forget I am dealing with more than meets the eye.

Proverbs 21:26 *"One who wanders from the path of understanding and good sense, will rest in the assembly of the dead."* What path is this? I am not walking on any path right now, am I? Jesus says I am, in fact, he clearly states that there are only two to choose from. A wide road and a narrow rocky path. (Matthew 7:13-14) He tells me the wide road, the easy road, the one most of us are traveling on, leads to destruction. The narrow path, the one rarely ever chosen, leads to a vibrant technicolor life; it leads the weary wide-eyed adventurer eventually to a land full of wonder that is just around the next corner. Is my daily wandering really that precarious? Will many of my friends and family end up walking with the assembly of the dead? Are they holding hands with hordes of demons and fanged monsters? Does aimlessness really involve that much danger? The Bible seems to think so.

Proverbs 15:11 *"Sheol and Abaddon lie open before the Lord; how much more the hearts of the children of man!"* Sheol, the place of the dead, and Abaddon, the great abyss that holds terrifying demons and dark angels, lie open, right this very moment, ready to swallow the unsuspecting average person like moths to a flickering flame. Most of us see the world as nothing more than a mundane existence. a boring routine, going to work, watching Netflix and taking an Advil and a few vitamins to stop joint pain as I get ready to slink into to bed on my $399 Serta mattress. Is Sheol widening her mouth under hundreds if not thousands of unsuspecting simpletons as they sleep in total ignorance? Is there more in this moment than simply paying bills and attending mindless parties? Is life a dangerous world? Is the Gospel that magical?

2. Both Evil and Good disguise themselves in the fairytale world. Buechner queries, "Who could guess that the little gray man asking for bread is a great magician who holds in his hands the power of life and death...Beasts talk and flowers come to life, and nothing is apt to be what it seems." For Christians, the man who was helplessly strung up on the cross, the despised one, the one whose name is daily used as a mere swear word of the cool and cunning, is getting ready this moment to return to the earth in his royal raiment. He will be beautiful to behold and mighty in word and deed. He is hidden, waiting, wanting people

to want him. But when he bursts on the scene he will shake the world, and everything that is not built on a sure foundation will crumble. And the one who looks beautiful now will be utterly shamed. The Devil will be defanged and humiliated, and those who follow the "god of this age" will be stricken silent and dumb, no more mocking, no more sinning in abundance, the adversary will be eating crow...and his army of followers, the arrogant and proud, the beautiful people of this current world, will be forced to choke on their own pride.

3. The fairytale is a world where the battle goes ultimately to the good, who live happily ever after, and wherein the long run everybody, good and evil alike, becomes known by his true name. I like how Frederick puts it here, "So great is the power of magic that even the less-than-good live happily ever after. It is the beast who becomes beautiful, the cowardly lion who becomes brave, the wicked sisters with their big feet and fancy ways who repent in the end and are forgiven. Happiness is not only inevitable, it is also endless." Christianity promises happily ever after as well. Revelation 22 says, "Let the evildoer still do evil, and the filthy still be filthy, and the righteous still do right, and the holy still be holy, Behold, I am coming soon, bringing my recompense with me, to repay each one for what he has done...Blessed are those who wash their robes so that they may have the right to the tree of life and they may enter the city by the gates."

We are walking among giants, people who have washed their robes in blood. Mighty men and women. And yet most of us yawn when we see them, or we cringed when we look into the bathroom mirror not seeing ourselves as we really are. The world to us is only gray, we feel like drops of water falling.

But this is not so!

Soon may seem like a relative word, something that seems far away, but I am not so sure. Soon I will close my eyes. Soon I will wake up in a bed that is mine, a soft bed, warm. Soon I will open my eyes and a familiar face will be looking at me, a face I will intimately know but have never seen before. I will know the voice. Soon I will also see my dad, alive, smiling, standing behind the face that is more beautiful than a sunrise, more alive than a summer day. I will feel like I did when as I boy I was standing with my dad by the edge of the shimmering water that was lapping up on Lake Erie beach. But it will be better. It will be soon.

Soon means I am near the edge of a world that is as close to me as a dream when one awakes. I am not a raindrop. I am an heir to the throne. Royalty hidden underneath the clothes of a commoner. There is more than meets the eye. My job is to live like magic is real.

I need to stop being bored.

So do you. Wake up the fairy tale is real. Jesus rose. Jesus is "I Am." Wake up!

Did you find this book insightful and encouraging in your walk with Christ? If so, you can read more blogs like this and purchase additional resources at:

www.christopherjweeks.com

ALSO AVAILABLE ON PAPERBACK

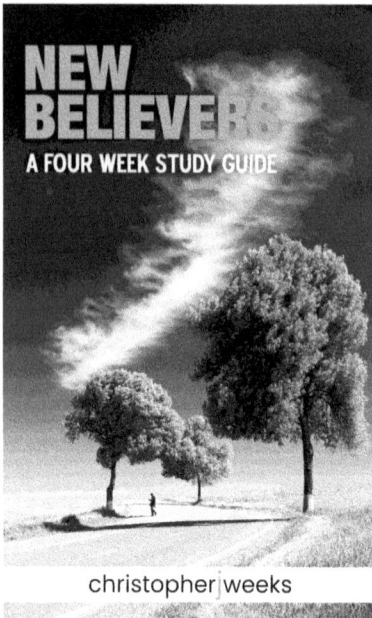

**NEW BELIEVERS
A Four-Week Study
Guide**

A clear and concise four-week study to help new believers sift through the emotional confusion that pervades our Christian culture and raises real-life questions that genuinely affect your eternal standing.

**BIBLE TOOLKIT
A New Believer's Guide
to the Bible**

Does the size of the Bible intimidate you? Have you ever wondered who writers like Habakkuk, Amos or Malachi are? And why are there four Gospels that seem to say different things about the same time period in Jesus' history? If you can answer yes to any of the above questions then this study guide is for you!

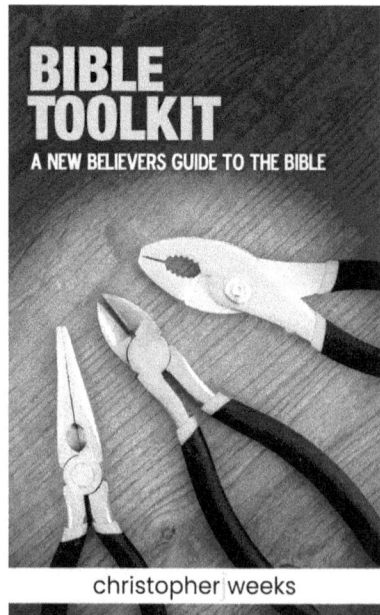

www.ingramcontent.com/pod-product-compliance
Lightning Source LLC
Chambersburg PA
CBHW072000040426
42447CB00009B/1417